MAVERICKS OF
GOLF

foreword by **Tom Watson**

MAVERICKS OF
GOLF

Behind Every Player Is
THE BUSINESS OF GOLF

JIM HANSBERGER

Another Quality Book Published By:

LEGACY BOOK PUBLISHING

1883 Lee Road, Winter Park, FL 32789

www.LEGACYBOOKPUBLISHING.com

Mavericks of Golf: Behind Every Player is the Business of Golf

Published by:
LEGACY Book Publishing
1883 Lee Road
Winter Park, Florida 32789
www.LegacyBookPublishing.com

© Jim Hansberger 2013.2014
Printed in the United States, 4th Printing
ISBN: 978-1-937952-52-5

Cover Design by Gabriel H.Vaughn

Table of Contents

Foreword

I like my office. In fact I love it. It just happens to be a golf course. On it I have played professional golf for more than four decades, for which I am very grateful and indebted.

In my "office" I have had the opportunity to meet so many fine and dedicated people who share my passion for this wonderful, diabolical game. One of these is Jim Hansberger, who contacted me in 1975 to see if I would be interested in joining his Ram Golf Company as a staff player to use his clubs and to carry the iconic red-and-white golf bag on Tour.

The initial question and concern I naturally had was whether or not I could change from the MacGregor clubs I had used for some seven years both as an amateur and after I turned professional. I had some relative success and, most importantly, a good comfort level playing with them. It was by no means an easy decision.

But after extensive testing of a number of Ram clubs, my final decision to change boiled down to my simple, but fundamental observation that Jim and his clubmakers truly understood how to build a quality balanced golf club. My transition from MacGregor thus became an easy one.

Over the next 22 years of my relationship with Ram, their commitment to use emerging, cutting edge technology to improve our clubs only confirmed my initial positive impression of Jim and Ram. In a tough, very competitive industry, they made their company into a success. I thank you, Jim, along with Gary Diehl, Ram's man on Tour, brothers Al and Lyle, Jerry Fortis, Terry Pocklington and, of course, Chuck Taft, my go-to club maker and all the others at Ram for the care you all put into your work and the relationships we built. We all created some lasting memories and had some great times together. It was a good run.

—Tom Watson

Preface

There has been so much technological development that has taken place over the years that has made the game of golf more enjoyable for the amateur. It has, however, been a challenge for the rules-making bodies to try and keep the equipment performance and the game the same as it was at its inception. That has been an almost impossible challenge.

This book is an attempt to show the history of golf and the history of the golf business from the perspective and personal experiences of an industry insider. The author/and or the author's family owned and/or operated the company known as Ram Golf Corporation for over 50 years. No other golf family business has ever hit that half century mark, although we would expect that Ping and the Solheim family will in the near future. During that time it has been an honor and a blessing to meet and spend time with so many wonderful people that have been a part of the game of golf and the business of golf. Whether they have been professional or amateur players, industry people or just people supportive to the game, they have been special.

Acknowledgment

I thank the many people who have worked with me and my family over the years to create the experiences that I have written about in this book. The family members that have encouraged me to detail some of the things we have done in the golf industry. Special thanks to some of my review experts like my sons Dave, Scott and Tom and also for the support from my daughter Tracy. Then there are my Tuscawilla Golf partners whose needling was I am sure intended to be helpful. The great recall of my brother Al and his wife Bev and son Gary were especially helpful. Gary Diehl was able to make corrections I could not have made alone. A special thank you, to my very long time friend, Chuck Rubin, for his many contributions. The help of wife Pola and her constant patience has been incredible.

CHAPTER 1

The Beginning-
And Then There Was Golf

It is commonly acknowledged that the game of golf began in Scotland around the late 1400s. We believe the early Scottish name was "gouf." Women have been involved in golf since the beginning. In fact, Mary Queen of Scots was accused of playing golf at Musselburgh in 1567 after her husband, Lord Darnley, was murdered, in which she was at least suspected of being involved. Musselburgh is actually the oldest playing course in the world and although Lord Darnley might resent it, the course is still there. It was probably not so good for ladies' golf, however, when 20 years later, Queen Elizabeth I of England had the Scottish Queen beheaded.

The most famous course in Scotland is St. Andrews, which was originally built as an 11-hole course along the sea. It was decided that some of the holes were too short so the course was modified in 1764 to 9 holes which were played as 9 holes "out" and 9 holes "in." Golf forevermore was to be an 18-hole game. The fact that a bottle of Scotch had 18 shots was just a coincidence. The first official rules were put together at St. Andrews by the Royal and Ancient (R & A) in 1744 and the basics have actually not changed all that much from those we play under today.

The St. Andrews golf course ran into financial difficulties and in 1799 it became a rabbit growing farm. Lucky for all, except the rabbits, it was bought back in 1805 to become St. Andrews again. Prior to 1863, there were no teeing areas, just the rule that said to tee off two to four club lengths from the prior green. At that time Old Tom Morris, the greenskeeper, put in teeing areas similar to what we have today. Initially there was not a standard size for the hole so it was decided to use the device that Royal Musselburgh had made to cut the hole into the green. That happened to be 4 ¼ inches and so in 1893 the R & A selected that as the standard and it still is today.

Golf spread rapidly through the UK and the British Empire and reached America about 100 years after the end of the War of Independence. Two of the first golf courses that were founded in America were St. Andrews Golf Club, Yonkers, New York and Chicago Golf Club in Downers Grove, Illinois. The St. Andrews Club was started as a 3-hole course in 1888. The first tee was by an apple tree and finished with a green built by the same apple tree. Thus the first American group of players was appropriately called "The Apple Tree Gang." The Chicago Golf Club of 1894 was the first 18-hole course in America. Chicago Golf Club later moved to another Chicago suburb, Wheaton, Illinois. The original course in Downers Grove is still there, but now as a 9-hole municipal course.

Members from five courses met in New York City that same year of 1894, to establish the association that would become the USGA. The five clubs represented were Chicago Golf Club; St. Andrews

Golf Club; The Country Club of Brookline, Massachusetts; Newport Country Club of Newport, Rhode Island; and Shinnecock Hills Country Club on Long Island. Thus, if there were to be a year for the official beginning of Golf in America it probably would be 1894.

Golf spread rapidly in America and by 1932 there were over 1100 golf courses. That was probably more than in all of the British Empire where it had all begun. An interesting aspect of American golf is that after each war was over, there was a growth in golf. A possible explanation is that as soldiers were finished with their wartime duties there was a bit of time for a relaxing sport and what could be less stressful than a relaxing game of competitive golf? Another explanation perhaps was that it was a good way to continue to make war but with golf clubs rather than guns. Still a battle, but nobody gets hurt.

Now that we had the game of golf and the places to play we needed the clubs and the ball to play with. The first Scottish golf balls were just round wooden balls that did not go very far. Next came the "feathery," which was a leather ball stuffed with goose feathers. Around 1850, a new solid rubber ball had been developed by Reverend Robert Patterson which was the "gutty." The first gutty was smooth, but it was discovered that as it was used and got some cuts it flew better. Putting a rough design around the ball helped it fly. This led to the dimple cover of today.

A big breakthrough came in 1898 when Coburn Haskell, of Cleveland, Ohio worked with B F Goodrich of Akron, Ohio to wind rubber thread around a solid core. Then by molding on a rubber cover, a lively ball was produced that had both a better feel and more controllable distance. That three-piece ball with a balata rubber cover became the standard design up to about 1965. The cover had to go thru a vulcanization process, usually with sulfur. The ball tended to have a limited shelf life and after a few months it would be less lively.

The first golf ball manufacturers tended to develop around Akron, Ohio or the Boston area. This included US Royal and BF Goodrich in Akron and the Worthington Golf Ball Company in Elyria, Ohio. The Acushnet Rubber Company, of New Bedford, Massachusetts, which became Titleist, started making golf balls in 1930. Spalding was even earlier, having started making golf balls in Chicopee, Massachusetts in 1895.

Over the years, the rules-making bodies in golf determined that the ball could not be less than 1.68 inches in diameter and the weight could not exceed 1.62 ounces. Many other golf ball rules were added as well such as dimple limitations and velocity and distance standards.

Some of the ball companies got into the club making side of the business as well, but most clubs were still being made by small independent clubmakers or by pros in their own shops. Early on, golf clubs had hickory shafts and wood heads made of persimmon wood. Iron heads were made of forged carbon steel that had to be given a protective coating such as chrome plating to prevent rust.

One of the companies that started to emerge as a leader in making clubs was Wilson Sporting Goods in Chicago. Primarily because of Wilson, Chicago became a hub for the emerging golf club business. This is what is referred to as a "cluster" in the auto and other industries. Companies of the same industry tend to group together because of the availability of skilled labor and component manufacturing companies. A former employee of Wilson was Nat Rosasco, who in 1929 started Northwestern Golf of Chicago. Sons Nat Jr. and Leroy expanded the company so that by the 1980s they could make the claim that they sold more golf clubs than any other company. Another Chicago offspring of Wilson was the Golfcraft Company that was started in 1945 by Ted Wooley and then moved to Escondido, California in 1957. Golfcraft was sold to Acushnet in 1969 and became the golf club division of Titleist.

MacGregor Golf began making clubs in Dayton, Ohio in 1897 and then moved to Cincinnati in 1946. They had a wonderful history with forged irons and persimmon woods. It was a company that had a great following with tour players including Jack Nicklaus, Byron Nelson, Johnny Miller, Greg Norman, Tom Weiskopf, Tony Penna, David Graham and Ben Hogan. MacGregor had a lot of ups and downs and became a part of the Brunswick Corporation in 1958.

Another one of the original golf companies was Burke Golf, which started making clubs in Newark, Ohio in 1910. This company was sold to Victor Comptometer in 1950 and moved to Morton Grove, Illinois in 1971 where it became PGA Golf and then Tommy Armour Golf.

"...The plant was in such a rough area of Chicago that, when shipments were ready, Lyle had to stand guard at night with both a pistol and a shotgun to protect them from being stolen."

CHAPTER 2

A FARM FAMILY BECOMES A GOLF FAMILY

In 1919, young Floyd Hansberger had returned to Minnesota from the fighting of World War I, had gotten married and began farming. By 1925, three children had been born. Times were tough and Floyd was known to say he "was so busy keeping the wolf from the door, the stork kept coming down the chimney." Farm machinery had been purchased on credit when disaster struck. A tornado came through, picked up the roof of the barn, and dropped it on the new machinery. Floyd was able to save himself and the two sons that were with him in the barn by pushing them into the gutter, when the bricks and timbers tumbled down on top of them. The good news was everybody was banged up, but alive. The bad news was Floyd would spend the next 15 years paying off the debt for the machinery he no longer had use of.

Shortly, three more children were born and through our teen years all six worked the farm and then found a way to work our way through college. The Hansberger brothers also, by necessity, learned to be hunters. Western Minnesota was pheasant country and ducks, pheasants, and an occasional deer became major supplements to the family food supply.

Lyle Hansberger finished his engineering education and found a job with an electrical appliance manufacturer in Chicago. Within a few months he decided it was time to start his own business. In 1946, at the age of 23, he founded Hansberger Tool and Die Company of Chicago. This company's operation included consulting and engineering, as well as the design and construction of specialized machines. The little company was contacted by George MacGregor Golf, a company making drivers for golf driving ranges. They needed some machines designed and built for their manufacturing operation. Soon, the George MacGregor Company was for sale and Lyle, along with older brother Bob and younger brother Al, raised the $5000 needed to buy them out. The brothers then formed a new company called Sportsmans Golf Corporation. A house on Hubbard

SPORTSMANS GOLF CORP 1948
1300 West Hubbard Street, Chicago, Illinois

Street in Chicago was acquired and, with a staff of seven, the fledgling company began producing a line of woods and irons. Because of a wartime law, manufacturing of nonessential products had been restricted and there had been little availability of balls and clubs. Now that the war was over, there was a pent-up demand for golf equipment.

The management structure of the company in the early years was Bob Hansberger as Chairman, Lyle as President, and Al Hansberger as Vice President. Al served in the Air Force and completed his education at Hamlin University. Bob received an engineering degree from the University of Minnesota and then served as an officer in the Navy. During that time, he taught engineering to Navy personnel. Once WW II was over, Bob went to Harvard for his MBA. By 1948, Bob was in Chicago working for Container Corp. As Chairman of Sportsmans, Bob was responsible for the board meetings which he would schedule for 5:30 AM so the meetings would not interfere with the workday.

As Lyle was getting the company underway there were US military forces scattered throughout the world and they needed some recreational activity. In many cases the troops would build makeshift golf courses with just a few holes. There were even reports of American and British POWs making a few golf holes in the German stalags. After the war ended in 1945, the military also built a few golf courses near bases. Clubs were needed, so the military asked for bids. Lyle was the low bidder at about $36 for five irons and two woods and a bag. This involved several thousand sets and the company was on the way. The plant was in such a rough area of Chicago that, when shipments were ready, Lyle had to stand guard at night with both a pistol and a shotgun to prevent them from being stolen. Since that time, a law has been passed in Chicago to prevent people from having a weapon.

1950 Jim and his college tuition

That law has disarmed the good guys, but has not had much effect in disarming the bad guys.

I was the youngest of the six siblings and, in high school, became active in exhibiting farm animals. One of those animals was a pig. The pig ended up a champion in the Minnesota State livestock show which enabled that 305-pound hog to be sold at auction for the big price of $244. Since the tuition for one year at the University of Minnesota was $180, the pig in effect sent me to college.

In 1951, I was invited to spend my high school vacation working at the Chicago factory. My bed was the office pullout sofa. Part of the duties was to be night watchman and as such I was given the 38 special. One night I was alerted to find that the rented warehouse across the street was being broken into. Running across the street and into the warehouse front door and firing while the thieves were running out the back was not very smart, but it was effective. The thieves had been surprised before they were able to load almost anything of value into their truck and make their getaway down the alley.

By this time the hickory shaft was a part of the past and steel shafts were readily available from True Temper and Union Hardware. Union Hardware actually introduced the first steel shaft and in 1924 the USGA ruled it "legal." For the grip, the method used was to wrap a paper underlisting on the shaft and then wrap and glue a strip of leather on to form the grip. This was a tedious process, but a pair of experienced grippers could do several hundred in a 10-hour shift. Lyle, with his engineering analysis, however, figured there had to be a better way.

Working with Cliff Spencer, Bill Junker and Tom Fawick and their rubber company in Akron, Ohio a process was developed to mold a rubber grip directly onto the shaft. These efforts in 1949 required molds and rubber which the Flexi Grip Company supplied and hot presses which Lyle built and installed in the basement of the house. Lyle found this new grip was ideal for the high volume, low cost operation he was developing. This allowed several thousand grips to be intalled per day. The initial name for this new molded-on grip was "Kushlite." Flexi Grip did not however have an easy time getting other manufacturers on board. As is often the case, the larger, more established manufacturers such as MacGregor, Spalding and Wilson all tended to ignore this new product. Many of the smaller more innovative companies like Burke, Kenneth Smith, Northwestern, and Hillerich and Bradsby were immediately interested.

By 1953, the process was changed to molding the grip on a mandrel (a removable rod) and then slipping it onto the shaft. The Akron Rubber Company, which had gone through various name changes, was now known as Fawick Flexi Grip. A popular motor oil at that time was "Gulf Pride" so Bill Junker decided "Golf Pride" would be a good name for a golf grip. The company hired touring pro Wally Ulrich to promote the new "slip on" Golf Pride grip on tour. Wally would take a set of pros' clubs to the trunk of his car, cut the worn leather grips off, glue in an extension plug and slip on the new rubber grips while the player waited. He did this for Tommy Bolt, who then went on to win the 1958 US Open. Chick Harbert had used Golf Pride grips to win the PGA Championship in 1954 and now with this second "major" the Golf Pride grip became a success. The "slip on" grip is now manufactured by many companies throughout the world, but the basic application process has changed little from the method developed way back in 1953. Interestingly, the Akron Rubber Company's original product that led them into making slip on golf grips was...condoms!

How They Are Made

Weight
Sorting

Face
Scoring

Hosel
Grinding

Milling
to Shape

Sole
Marking

Weight
Grinding

In the early years, nearly all iron golf heads were made by the drop forging method. This process consisted of making a large progressive die with multiple positions, Rough, Middle and Finish. A bar of iron would be heated red hot and then held in each position until it was pounded into shape.

Al Cornell of Cornell Forging, Chicago, and Marty Hoffman of Hoffman Die Products, Memphis, were the main suppliers to the golf industry. The limitations of this process were that the product arrived at the clubmaker in a fairly raw form and required a lot of skill to grind and polish it into a golf club. There were only a few companies that had the skilled craftsmen to grind the forgings to make clubs of sufficient quality and the weight grinding needed to make a professional grade golf iron. The only companies in the 1960s and '70s that seemed to be able to do this consistently well were MacGregor, Wilson and Ram.

The process of stamping in the face scoring and the marking on the iron heads was a huge bottleneck in the manufacturing process. This was especially true with Lyle's concept of a high volume, low cost operation. The old method of doing the face scoring lines had been to hold a chisel by hand and then hit that chisel with a heavy mallet. This was an obviously dangerous and time consuming job. A machine had been developed that would push in all those scoring lines at one time with high pressure, but it was very expensive and cumbersome. Lyle was able to buy a much more versatile hydraulic roll marking machine and then modify it with special fixtures so that it would not only roll in those scoring lines, but then could be used for the individual sole and back markings as well. This was a major advancement for the company and production and sales rapidly increased. Lyle was the first in the industry with many of these early manufacturing advances and they soon found their way into other clubmakers' factories.

Once on a late afternoon after the employees had gone home, brother Al was in the office meeting with a new sales rep from one of the suppliers. During their conversation, a man in coveralls came in with mops and cleaning materials and proceeded with his daily routine to clean the office and washrooms. The sales rep was so impressed with the professionalism of the worker that he remarked to Al how well the cleaning man did his job. "Lyle does his other jobs of President and Chief Engineer well also" was Al's reply.

KROYDON THUNDERBOLT IRON

CHAPTER 3

Rapid Growth

By 1952, the company had reached $1,000,000 in annual sales and had expanded into the office secretary's house next door. By 1956, the company had grown too large for both houses and a new 25,000-square-foot modern office and factory was built in Melrose Park, a suburb of Chicago. The Kroydon club line was added in 1957 and several million clubs were made under that brand. A professional line under the name Bristol was added in 1960. The company was growing at a rate of almost 30% per year and had to keep expanding its facilities. The plant was doubled in size in 1958 and additional construction would be done to double again in 1961 to a total of 104,000 square feet.

In the early 50's the brothers had realized that having pro endorsements would help the club business. The problem was the fledgling company did not have the funds for this. The given names, of each of the four brothers were Robert Vail, William Lyle, Allan Payne, and James Richard. The four new "creative" pro lines became "Bobby Vail", "Bill Lyle", "Al Payne", and "Jimmy Richard". They sold amazingly well until real pro relationships could be achieved.

Bob Hansberger had taken a new job in 1956 as President of Boise Payette Lumber Company. Within a year he had merged the company with the Cascade Lumber Company to form Boise Cascade. With his management, that company would grow to over 3 billion in sales. One of the divisions of Boise Cascade that was sold is now known as Office Max. Bob also served on the President's Business Advisory council under President Ford. An interesting side point is that Gerald Ford's family owned the Ford Paint and Varnish Company of Grand Rapids, Michigan. Dick Ford, who was President Ford's younger brother was the go-to guy for much of the materials used by the industry to finish wood golf clubs.

In the late '50s and early '60s, many specialty golf products were developed by Sportsman including the Wizard putter line in partnership with George Low. The model stamped "George Low Wizard 600" was used by Jack Nicklaus to win many of his majors. If you can find one of the originals with the mark "Sportsman," it is worth $20,000 or more to collectors. George Low was the first professional that the company had worked with on an endorsement basis and it was a challenging experience. At that time George was known as "America's Guest" and a book was published by that title. He earned that name because he did not seem to have his own home. He would just move in with people. That included Bing Crosby at times or so George would say. While he was in Chicago he usually stayed with Joe Jemsek, the owner of the Chicago courses of Cog Hill and St. Andrews. George actually was an extremely good putting coach and

SPORTSMAN

George Low

A NEW CONCEPT IN PUTTERS

The most solid touch ever put in a golf club. You've never had the sensation of "Firm Feel" that you'll get when you use a "Wizard" putter. Designed for Sportman's Golf Corp. by George Low, the fabulous putting wizard, these putters at last give you the opportunity to *control* your putting. They are the product of 20 years of research and experience on tour. The Wizard putters combine *all* the features necessary in top quality putters: The most successful and accepted head designs over the past 20 years. Consistency in manufacturing. Straight, true lines that address the ball with authority and confidence. A "firm feel" fluted shaft that allows consistency in putting. A tight wound flat top calfskin grip for best holding quality and the new rectangular (Dupont Delrin) inserted hitting face for the most sensitive touch you'll find in any putter today.

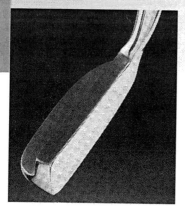

George Low and the Wizard 600 Putter

worked with many touring professionals over the years.

George loved to play the horses and he had found an interesting way to make extra money for his bets. He would spend time in the club bar and find a player who thought he could putt pretty well. George would challenge him that he could putt better with his shoe than the guy could with his putter. What the "pigeon" did not know is that George could putt better than anyone just using his shoe. Before long George would have 50 bucks in his pocket. The George Low Wizard series putters were developed with George, but did not become popular until several years later when the 600 model, with George's help, found its way into Jack Nicklaus's bag.

By this time, I, as the youngest Hansberger brother, had completed my engineering and business education at the University of Minnesota. I started working for Motorola in Chicago as a project engineer building specialty machines and doing similar work at the golf plant at night. By 1960, my brothers offered me the opportunity to come into the golf company full time and to become a part owner. The first work they assigned was to develop a machine that could be used to semi-automatically bore the hole in the iron forging and prepare it for assembly with the tapered steel shaft. There was a machine on the market at that time made by Kingsbury Machines that cost about $30,000 with fixtures. We were able to design and build a machine including the fixtures for under $3,000. Later a second machine was built to the same specs and both machines remained in operation for over 20 years. The next three years were spent under Lyle's tutorship building

GOLF CLUB SPECIFICATIONS

LENGTH

IRONS	LONG	STANDARD	LADIES
1	40	39	—
2	39½	38½	37½
3	39	38	37
4	38½	37½	36½
5	38	37	36
6	37½	36½	35½
7	37	36	35
8	36½	35½	34½
9	36	35	34
PW	36	35	34
SW	36	35	34
WOODS			
1	44	43	42
3	43	42	41
4	42½	41½	40½
5	42	41	40

IRONS	LIE MENS	LIE LADIES	LOFT MENS	LOFT LADIES
1	56.0°	—	18.0°	—
2	56.7°	57.6°	21.0°	21.0°
3	57.5°	58.4°	24.3°	24.3°
4	58.2°	59.1°	27.8°	27.8°
5	59.0°	60.0°	31.5°	31.5°
6	60.0°	61.0°	35.3°	35.3°
7	60.9°	61.9°	39.2°	39.2°
8	61.7°	62.6°	43.3°	43.3°
9	62.6°	63.5°	47.5°	47.5°
PW	62.6°	63.5°	51.6°	51.6°
SW	62.6°	63.5°	56.7°	56.7°
WOODS				
1	54.0°	55.5°	11.0°	12.5°
3	55.6°	56.0°	16.5°	16.5°
4	56.0°	56.5°	19.2°	19.2°
5	56.3°	57.0°	22.0°	22.0°

Specialty Machines and Club Specs

machines and fixtures to automate as much of the golf club operations as possible.

One of the early experiences at the company was Thanksgiving in 1960. On the day before the holiday, Al and I were informed by Lyle that the company had been notified that its boiler system area needed to be enclosed for safety reasons and that we all would be spending Thanksgiving building the needed cement block wall. At 3 o'clock in the afternoon on Thanksgiving Day, the job was completed and the Hansberger crew was allowed to go home for Thanksgiving dinner. It was at this point that the realization came that being a business owner was going to require a bit of extra commitment and sacrifice.

Tommy Bolt had won the US Open in 1958 and in the early '60s he joined the company as a staff professional. Tommy was recognized as having one of the "sweetest" swings in golf. Tommy, however had a well-known temper and was nicknamed "Terrible Tom" or "Thunderbolt." Tommy's mentor was Ben Hogan, who was quoted as saying "If we could've screwed another head on his shoulders, Tommy Bolt could have been the greatest that ever played." Tom was really a great guy to be with, at least off the course. He had a great sense of humor and some of his club throwing was for the galleries' entertainment. Some of Tommy Bolt's classic quotes were "Always throw clubs ahead of you; that way you won't waste any energy going back to pick them up." And "Never break your driver and putter in the same round." Golf writers at the time came up with the story that as Tommy was ready to hit his second shot on the 18th hole he asked the caddy what club to hit. The caddy said "a #2 iron because that's the only one we have left." Tommy was always a great pro-am partner. In one hospital charity outing, when asked how his partners played, Tommy said "I saw more strokes out there than you would see in the hospital."

Sister Dorothy Hansberger also graduated from the University of Minnesota. She had married Oscar

Austad and they were raising their family in Sioux Falls, South Dakota. Oscar traveled through several surrounding states as an insurance adjuster. He and Al Hansberger had decided in 1963 that mail order golf equipment sales could be developed into a business. Oscar would then stop into local banks or attorneys' offices on his travels and take orders for golf clubs. The order would then be passed on to the Austad shipping department. That was Dorothy in the garage, which by this time had become a warehouse. When the business grew too large for the garage, Oscar leased a building and hired a small staff. Soon the business was grossing over one million dollars a year and Oscar finally decided it was safe to quit his day job.

They regularly printed a mail order golf catalog and Austad Golf became the largest customer for the Post Office in South Dakota. As Austads continued to grow they brought in additional golf brands and became the largest mail order golf supplier in the United States. Oscar Austad also found time to serve several years as a state senator in South Dakota. In honor of this title, the company produced a special series of clubs for the Austad Company called the "Senator." They actually sold quite well. After Oscar retired, his son Dave established the Austad retail golf store chain throughout the Midwest.

"...Ram's early introduction of the Surlyn cover ball proved to be so advantageous that the Ram golf ball business virtually doubled every year for four years"

CHAPTER 4

The Golf Company
Becomes Ram

A growing golf ball manufacturer called The Golf Development Company of Bay City, Michigan was acquired by Sportsmans in 1964 and in 1965 this was incorporated into a new 107,000 square foot state-of-the-art manufacturing complex in Pontotoc, Mississippi. The city of Pontotoc was very welcoming and went out of its way to provide services. Sportsman was to provide many jobs for the community. This was a successful quid pro quo for everyone as the company became the largest employer in the area.

The golf ball company that had been purchased owned several trademarks including the name Ram. The company was just getting into tour endorsements and when providing staff bags to the players there was an obvious advantage to having a short name. In 1967, the corporate name was officially changed to Ram Golf Corporation and now there was a big bold RAM on Tommy Bolt's bag. Golf on TV was the new way to show your brand and the new RAM name was getting big time exposure.

As a part of the purchase of the golf ball company their staff professional, Tony Lema, became a part of the staff for golf balls. Tony had just beaten Jack Nicklaus to win the British Open at St. Andrews in

Ready to tee it up in the Music City Open are (left to right) Lawrence Welk, Perry Como, Chet Atkins and Ram's Tommy Bolt. Como, an excellent and avid golfer, was on the winning team.

1964 and was very popular worldwide. Tony bought champagne for all the press after one tournament and thereafter he became "Champagne Tony." With the plans to promote the new ball program, Tony was going to be a big part of the 1966 product line. Then tragedy struck. Tony and his wife had chartered a plane to fly them from Akron to Chicago for an exhibition. The plane crashed as it was coming in to land in Lansing, Illinois and all aboard were killed. The company now had a big decision to make. It was decided that the proper, ethical and responsible thing to do was to stop everything. All advertising and promotion was scrapped and packaging materials destroyed. It was a very sad time for the business and for the golf world.

Terry Pocklington, a chemical engineer originally educated in England, joined the company and immediately started to create a totally new golf ball product using a DuPont material called "Surlyn." This provided an unbelievable golf ball cover in that it would not cut, as did the balata-covered ball that was in use at that time. It provided greater distance for the average player. The big problem initially was cold cracking. A testing device was built by Lyle that was a big metal box with steel baffles welded to the inside walls. Golf balls would be put in a freezer to bring their temperature down to about 10 degrees Fahrenheit. The golf balls would then be driven into the box at high speeds with an air cannon, and if they could survive the impacts against the baffles they should survive normal play.

The first ones did not and so by mixing different DuPont Surlyns a blend was developed by Terry that solved the cold cracking issues. The first commercial Surlyn ball was the Ram 3D. It was advertised as Distance, Durability, and Dependability. Ram's early introduction of the Surlyn cover ball proved to be so advantageous that the Ram golf ball business virtually doubled every year for four years until the competition caught up. Even after that, the continued growth in the ball business was exceptional.

One of the great showman golfers joined RAM in 1966. That would have to be Doug Sanders. Doug was always impeccably dressed and everything had to match. The RAM staff bags at that time were made with a very colorful and expensive DuPont material called "Corfam." A special removable panel was built into Doug's bag so that he could change the panel to match his shoes. He had arranged with his shoe company to make the shoes out of the same Corfam. Doug even went to the point of having his socks dyed to match the shoe color. Doug had a short fast backswing that was unusual, but effective. He won many PGA Tour events and at the British Open at St. Andrews in 1970 Doug had a one shot lead over Jack Nicklaus with a two-and-a-half-foot putt to win on the 18th hole. As Doug set up to knock it in, he saw something in his line so he reached down to brush it aside. He then realized it was a small piece of dead grass that was still attached which a player is not allowed to remove. This so unnerved him that he never properly readjusted himself and missed the putt. An 18-hole playoff was scheduled for the next day and Jack won with his Sportsman George Low Wizard 600 putter.

CHAPTER 5

The Golf Industry Expands

The 1960s were great growth years for golf with almost 4000 new courses opening up in this decade. Television was popularizing the game, and so was Arnold Palmer. He was an exciting player who had a lot to do with golf's becoming more of a sport for the general public. Many of the new courses were either public or municipal, which made golf more accessible and affordable. Nearly all golf companies were doing well and most were growing at a 10% to 20% rate. This was probably the most profitable decade ever for golf equipment manufacturers. This was also a product of the Eisenhower era (1953-1961) and not only did he popularize the game because of his own play, but his administration was very business friendly and energized the golf business as well. This was also a period where the government stayed out of the way and it was easy to start and grow a new business. The following administrations of Kennedy, Johnson, Nixon and Ford that together ran from 1961 to 1977 were all quite positive for the economy as well. The increasingly excessive government regulations that came in after that are not likely to ever allow so much entrepreneurship again.

Many of the golf operations of today got their start in the business friendly '50s and '60s. One example was an engineer working for the

Environmental Protection Agency by the name of Carl Paul. He first started repairing clubs in his New Jersey garage in 1967. He then started sourcing components and printing a small catalog for golf repair shops. Carl continued working for the EPA while his wife Barbara took the orders. Carl finally quit his government job, and moved his company, now called Golfsmith, to Austin, Texas. There he was joined by brother Frank in what was a new and rapidly expanding golf business. Carl was very instrumental in converting many golf repair shops into custom-fit clubmakers.

Golf-related businesses were naturally expanding as well. These included air travel, lodging, rental cars, entertainment, food and beverage, apparel, and real estate. The golf effect was especially powerful in the winter vacation destinations of California, Arizona, and Florida, where golf courses became a prime factor in real estate development. It was estimated that the golf and golf-related industry had grown to over 20 billion dollars by 1970 and continued to grow to over 60 billion by the year 2000.

During the '60s I began attending tour events to promote Ram products. Karsten Solheim and I met for the first time while both of us were working with players. Although Karsten was in his fifties and I was in my thirties, we found we had a lot in common. Often we scheduled trips together so we could work with tour players on Monday and Tuesday, play golf together on Wednesday and fly home Wednesday evening. Since Karsten was promoting Ping putters and I was promoting Ram irons we could work with the same player without conflict. The products that we each were offering were not only different materials, but were made differently as well. The Ping putter was originally sand-cast beryllium copper while the Ram iron was forged carbon steel and then chrome plated. I found Karsten to be not only creative but also very good at engineering concepts and I developed a lot of respect for his honesty and sincerity. Karsten's other characteristic of perseverance worked to his advantage. One week he would offer to fit a player with his new Ping putter and be turned down. A couple of weeks later he would be back and offer the putter again. Eventually, the player would give up and try the putter.

In 1967, Julius Boros won the Phoenix Open with the Ping Anser putter and said, "The putter looks like a bunch of nuts and bolts welded together, but the ball goes in the hole." In 1969, George Archer did the same at the Masters. From then on the tables were turned and players were asking for the putter. A big part of Karsten's success was his wife, Louise. She handled the finances and kept the family and the business together while Karsten did the designing and promotion. They were a very strong Christian family. This carried through in the way they ran their company and raised their four children, Louis, Sandra, Allan and John, all of whom went to work for the company.

Karsten started doing some international travel and Louise frequently went on the trips with him. On one of these trips they visited the Solheim family relatives in Norway. Unfortunately, there was an auto accident in their rented car and Karsten received some minor injuries. About this time Karsten grew a beard which became a bit of a family trademark when he started doing commercials to promote Ping products.

During one of our rounds of golf in the late '60s, Karsten announced that he had a new set of irons that he would like me to try. The clubs were investment cast and had an unfinished dull look. When I asked why they were not polished, Karsten explained that he did not have an iron polishing setup and so he planned to bring them to market with just the tumbled unfinished look. His intention was to cast the clubs with a total finished shape so little grinding would be necessary. He also made the clubs with a stronger loft so in effect his 6 iron was actually a 5 iron. This made the player believe the club design was producing more distance.

After hitting several shots with them, I found they hit very well. I was skeptical about the unfinished look and the lack of flexibility in grinding. Karsten, in his usual manner said, "I am going to try to fit players just the way they are." It was, however, a tough sell on tour. He first started having a positive response on the #1 and #2 irons. The reason was the bigger perimeter weighted head made them more forgiving than the small forged blade. As Lee Trevino famously said, when you see lightning on the golf course hold up a one iron because "Even God can't hit a one iron." As usual, Karsten's persistence paid off and Ping became one of the top selling irons in golf.

The 1969 PGA Championship was to be held at the NCR Club in Dayton, Ohio. When I arrived to showcase Ram products with tour players, Ram staff pro Bob Rosburg advised me that a young pro by the name of Ray Floyd was available for a possible staff arrangement. We then got together with Ray

Dave Hill

Doug Sanders

Ram Staff Members in the Early '70s

Gene Littler

Bob Rosburg

Tom Shaw

Ray Floyd

Ram Staff Members in the Early '70s

Judy Rankin

Cesar Sanudo

and agreed to work something out. Ray also agreed to carry a Ram staff bag for the tournament. The only bag available was the 9-inch staff bag that I was using to carry samples. Ray proceeded to use that bag while winning the tournament, and thus he started his Ram staff career with the Ram bag receiving huge television coverage. The next year at the Crosby Pro-Am tournament in Pebble Beach, Ray invited me to join him at a party at Clint Eastwood's house in Carmel Valley. It turned out to be a true Hollywood blast and Ray and Clint continued to be Crosby pro-am partners for another 20 years.

Golf was growing in popularity and Ram was becoming a more recognized brand throughout the world. The bad news was that golf equipment was becoming a profitable and easy product for thieves to dispose of. Each morning a local truck line would drop off a large semi trailer at Ram's Melrose Park shipping dock. That trailer would then be filled during the day with shipments. At the end of the day the trailer would be picked up and Ram's shipments would be on the way. At the appointed time on one particular day a rogue truck backed in, hooked up to the trailer and sped away with $100,000 in golf shipments. The theft was quickly discovered by the driver of the legitimate truck coming in and he radioed all trucks in the area and the police. Because the trailer contained interstate shipments, the FBI was called in. Within 12 hours, the FBI had located the trailer inside a building less than two miles away. Thanks to the efforts of the FBI, the entire trailer load was recovered and the Chicago gang apprehended.

"...As we approached the first tee, I said to my weathered Scottish caddy, "What do you think about this weather?" expecting him, of course, to agree with my concerns. Instead he replied, "It is a bit better today." Welcome to Scottish golf!!"

CHAPTER 6

The Industry Develops and Bonds

This was also a period where there was a great deal of friendship in the industry. Most golf companies were privately owned and everyone was making money and working on growing their businesses without having to do it at the expense of others. In 1936, the National Golf Foundation (NGF) had been formed by Herb and Joe Graffis, who were the publishers of Golfdom Magazine. They were able to convince six golf manufacturers to come up with a combined total of $17,000 to fund the startup. Those six manufacturers were Spalding, Wilson, MacGregor, Hillerich and Bradsby, US Royal, and the Worthington Golf Ball Company. The sole purpose was to promote golf. They proposed this in three basic ways 1) more golf courses, 2) more players, and 3) better utilization of courses. This organization to this day has been very successful and has continued to develop more and better ways to achieve these goals. The NGF is also the primary source for research information on golf courses and golf-related business.

David Heuber joined the NGF as a field rep in the '70s and then went to work for Deane Beaman as a VP of Marketing for the PGA Tour. When Don Rossi retired from the NGF in 1983, David came back as President and CEO of the NGF. Shortly after that, the Japanese company Cosmos World bought the Ben Hogan Company and recruited David to be President and CEO. Later, they acquired the Pebble Beach Golf Course and David became involved in their golf course management and development projects. More recently, David has received a PhD from Clemson University and for his dissertation he wrote a highly informative document on ownership and development of golf courses.

I became involved with the NGF and served on its Board of Directors for nearly 25 years starting in the late 1960s. The Executive Director at that time was Don Rossi who had great success at having competitors work together for the common good of golf. Various associations were formed within the NGF umbrella. Examples were Golf Course Superintendents Association (GCSA), Golf Course Builders Association (GCBA), Golf Course Owners Association (GCOA), Golf Club Manufacturers Association (GCMA), and Golf Ball Manufacturers Association (GBMA). Some of the officer positions that I served in include president of the GBMA and treasurer of the NGF. Other officers over the years included Dean Cassell, executive VP, Titleist; George Dickerman, president of Spalding; Bob MacNally, president, PGA Golf/Tommy Armour; David Heuber, president, Ben Hogan Co; Joe Phillips, VP, Wilson; and Allan Solheim, VP, Karsten Manufacturing. When David Heuber took the Ben Hogan position, Dr. Joe Bettis, who headed up the NGF research operations, was well prepared to be his replacement.

During the '60s and the '70s, the association for sports including golf was the National Sporting

Goods Association (NSGA). The NGF had not yet grown into being a completely stand alone association and so the NGF meetings were conducted as a part of the annual NSGA gathering. There would be discussions of industry conditions and a golf tournament. Each year there would be a regular foursome of Dan Sheehan of Cast Metal Alloys, Jim Butz of PGA Golf, Karsten Solheim of Ping, and myself. Dan Sheehan, a former NFL player and the comedian of the group, decided on one par 3 to tell a joke while waiting for the green to clear. As Dan was still talking, the green cleared and Karsten hit his shot. Dan then walked over to his good friend Karsten, put his hands on Karsten's shoulders and said, "Please, don't hit when I'm talking." It was the usual day of good times and lots of laughs.

The PGA show began as a small affair in Dunedin, Florida in 1954. In those days it was little more than a few salesmen opening the trunks of their cars and showing their wares to the club professionals that happened to be in Florida for the winter. By 1957, it became large enough to rent a tent. From 1963 to 1974, the show moved between St. Lucie, Florida and Palm Beach Gardens, Florida, still in a tent, but the tent was getting larger. It finally went inside in 1975 at the Disney Contemporary Hotel in Orlando. Then, after a short time in Miami Beach, the show found a permanent home in 1985 at the huge Orlando Convention Center. During the 1960s, as the PGA show grew in attendance, golf companies exhibited at the NSGA shows and meetings less and the PGA show more. Golf had grown large enough to stand on its own.

In fact the PGA show that began with a few car trunks in 1954 had grown by 1990 to take over 1,000,000 square feet of exhibit space. The NGF had also become more independent and now held its annual meeting as a part of the PGA show.

The original home of golf became of more interest to Ram as a market opportunity. With this in mind, I traveled to Scotland in 1966. Upon arrival, our new potential partner for the UK, Bob Dickson, and I went to Gleneagles Golf Course for a round of golf. The day was cold, rainy, windy and just plain miserable. My thoughts were "no human in his right mind will ever be playing golf in these conditions." It was decided, however, that we would proceed. As we approached the first tee, I said to my weathered Scottish caddy, "What do you think about this weather?"expecting him, of course, to agree with my concerns. Instead he replied, "It is a bit better today." Welcome to Scottish golf!!

The Gleneagles Golf Club at that time had three courses. The Kings course, the Queens course, and the "Wee Course" which was a short 9-hole layout. The land used for this original Wee course has gone through changes over the years and today it is part of the PGA Centennial course layout for the 2014 Ryder Cup matches, where Tom Watson will captain the US team.

After surviving the round of golf, the new partners visited a metal casting company that was using the "lost wax" process to cast stainless steel golf heads for the UK market. This process had the advantage of having all the markings and face scoring lines already done when the head comes out of the ceramic mold. An order was placed for a head design called the "World Tour" to be cast, finished and shipped to Ram in Chicago. That was believed to be the first investment cast irons to be offered in the US market. This is the same process that Karsten Solheim perfected in manufacturing the first Ping clubs after he went into the golf business full time in 1967.

Since this was the first instance of finished golf club heads arriving in the US, a ruling needed to be made by US customs. Were the imported heads a finished product which would mean they would require a "country of origin" mark at retail or were they only a component of a US manufactured product? The ruling was made that they were a component, and ever after heads that are completely finished overseas and are only assembled in the US do not require a country of origin marking on the clubs at retail. Today, the majority of all brands of clubs are assembled in the US with primarily foreign components and carry no marking or in some cases may have a sticker saying "Assembled in the USA."

The history of Golf Pride grips is a good example of the history of manufacturing in the United States. From the startup date in 1949, all grips were made in Akron, Ohio and the company grew and prospered. The rubber industry in Akron was heavily unionized and so the workers at Golf Pride became unionized as well. When the owners saw an opportunity to sell the company to The Eaton Corporation in 1968, they did so. The high cost of labor drove the company out of Akron and a new state-of-the-art plant was built in Laurinburg, North Carolina. Golf Pride wanted to showcase this new operation and invited industry leaders to a tournament at the Country Club of North Carolina at Pinehurst. This tournament was held for the first time in 1969 and continued on an annual basis on thru the '70s. Golf Pride also invited several pros to be a part of the activities. Two of the greats that came were Tommy Bolt and Sam Snead. Now Tommy and Sam did not get along well. As everyone knows, Sam in his later years had become quite

Golf Pride Pro Am 1971
Dave Stockton, Jim Hansberger, Jerry O'Neil, Henry McGill

bald and always wore a hat. After he had finished his round, he had gone into the locker room and removed the fedora to reveal his white top just has Tommy walked in. Tommy took one look and said "Hey there's old nude nob." Sam had remarkable composure in managing to ignore Tommy.

The labor cost was much more reasonable in North Carolina and by 1992 Eaton had built an additional 100,000 square feet and had over 750 employees. Labor costs continued to rise, however, and today that plant is closed and all Golf Pride manufacturing transferred to Taiwan and Thailand. It is disappointing that thousands of manufacturing companies have found it necessary to take labor-intensive operations out of America to remain competitive.

Lyle Hansberger, Gene Littler and Al Hansberger
1960

CHAPTER 7

US and Foreign Markets Grow

Gene Littler had won the US Open in 1961 and joined Ram's staff in the late '60s. Gene's swing was so smooth and consistent he became known as "Gene the Machine." Ram had started to develop the Japanese market and found it to be a growing and enthusiastic market for American golf clubs. I, along with our Japan distributor, arranged an exhibition at both a Tokyo driving range and a golf course outside the city, with Gene Littler. Gene did a wonderful job and was very well received by the Japanese public. Both of us did extensive golf press interviews. This trip did a lot to introduce Ram products to the Japanese market.

In 1972, Gene was diagnosed with cancer of the lymph nodes and surgery was performed. With lots of dedication and swimming exercise at his La Jolla, California home, Gene was able to rebuild his arm and shoulder muscles and, within about 6 months, he was back playing and winning. Gene's career was long and successful with 29 PGA tour wins and eight senior Tour wins. He is definitely one of the real heroes of golf.

The main method of shipping within the golf industry during the 1960s was either by parcel post for small shipments or by truck for anything of any size. This presented a problem for all golf companies, because the delay in getting the product to the customer could easily take 10 days to two weeks or more. The solution was that most companies opened warehouses around the country to shorten the time. Ram opened warehouses in New York, Charlotte, Los Angeles, and Dallas. This along with the main manufacturing locations in Illinois and Mississippi reduced shipping time to any continental US location to two or three days, which definitely helped in the growth of business. After a few years, however, the cost of operating a warehouse in California became prohibitive. The state had imposed a floor tax on all inventory and so, like many other businesses, Ram relocated its warehouse across the border to Reno, Nevada. The same good service could be provided, but without the California tax. This tax law caused California to lose a lot of jobs and thus reduced tax revenue. This was a good example of the unwise tax policies so common with the anti-business governments of states like California, Illinois and Michigan.

The 1969 British Open Championship was contested at Lytham St. Annes and a meeting was scheduled between Orville Moody and myself to discuss "Sarge's" joining the Ram staff. Sarge had just won the 1969 US Open and looked a good bet to win the British as well. The meeting was planned to take place in the locker room as soon as he finished the day's round. During that round, however, on one of the early holes Sarge had pushed his drive out of bounds and over the adjoining railroad tracks on the right. When he did it the second time he had gone from contender to well back. Unfortunately, he was so devastated by the situation that the meeting was cancelled and never rescheduled. He went on to finish tied for 16th with Tony Jacklin taking the trophy. Also, unfortunately, Sarge never won a second PGA tour event. When he reached the Senior Tour, however, he did very well, winning a total of 11 senior events.

The sixth Hansberger sibling was sister Jean Hansberger, who was married to Al Norby and was living in Charlotte, NC. With the opening of a new sales office and warehouse in Charlotte, Al Norby joined Ram as regional manager. Later they would move to Chicago and Al Norby would become the director of corporate administration for Ram. Now, with Jean's husband in the company, all six Hansberger siblings had an active part in Ram Golf.

The Golden Ram ball was introduced in 1970 and was involved in winning many tournaments by Ram's Staff Professionals including Gene Littler, Tom Shaw, Nancy Lopez and Tom Watson. The "Surlyn" cover material that Ram had first

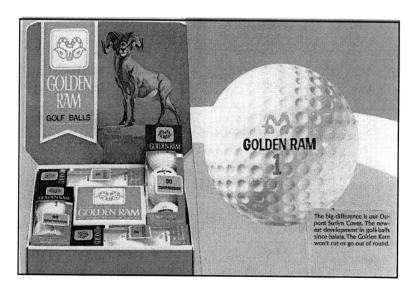

The big difference is our Du-pont Surlyn Cover. The new-est development in golf balls since balata. The Golden Ram won't cut or go out of round.

introduced on a golf ball in 1966 became the basic cover material that 70% or more of all wound golf balls manufactured worldwide were using by 1972.

True Temper had become the leading manufacturer of steel golf shafts and in 1963, the long time general manager of True Temper's golf division, Gurdon Leslie, contracted with Batelle Memorial Institute to develop a robot that would duplicate a human golf swing. The project engineer for the machine was George Manning, a 28-year-old mechanical engineer. After much research George chose Byron Nelson's swing as the pattern, and thus this machine became known as the "Iron Byron." George said he chose Byron because of his swings "efficiency and consistency." The machine provided for a regular driver to be fastened into the machine and then through electro mechanical devices and controls the device would swing the club just like Byron. The machine was made available to True Temper customers for testing and most manufacturers, including Ram, ended up buying their own. In 1966, shortly after the machine was perfected, George went to work for True Temper and then in 1972 when Gurdon Leslie retired George Manning replaced him as general manager. The USGA also bought one and ended up using it to set the standards for golf ball distance limitations. Prior to the use of this machine, the USGA tested golf balls to limit ball velocity to 250 feet per second. This machine allowed the USGA to add an "overall distance limit." This was set up to be 317 yards with a driver head speed of 120 miles per hour. Obviously, there were many other specifications on the testing, but these were the basics.

Adjustments could be made and golf ball manufacturers, like Ram, found that with this machine, the effect on distance with different ball constructions could be determined quite accurately. It was possible to see the effect of loft angle, swing speed and shaft flex on golf ball distance as well. This also provided many opportunities for testing the effect of different shaft materials and club head weight distribution and materials. The Iron Byron was a bargain at $250,000.

While the Iron Byron was being built, the "Banshee," a 25-foot sailboat set off from South Africa with a young South African engineer and his friend with the destination of America. They survived the journey with many harrowing experiences. The young engineer was Frank Thomas who went to work for Shakespeare where he developed the first graphite golf shaft. Shakespeare, however, decided to concentrate on fishing equipment. Frank then moved to the USGA and became their technical director in 1974 and remained so for 26 years. During that time, Frank designed and built the USGA testing equipment for golf balls and golf clubs and became the go-to guy on technical issues for the rules of golf. This was probably the toughest job in golf, but Frank handled it well and became one of the most respected people in golf.

Frank not only was an innovator himself, but with his position at the USGA he saw a lot of "off the wall" creations. This brings to mind two industry innovators. John Riley started by working with Karsten Solheim in the early 1960s before Ping was yet born. He then formed a company that

GENERAL OFFICES & DISTRIBUTION CENTER
ELK GROVE VILLAGE, ILLINOIS

MIDWEST FACTORY: MELROSE PARK, ILLINOIS

MID-SOUTH FACTORY: PONTOTOC, MISSISSIPPI

became Lynx which Carl Ross ended taking over. From there he set up a small California company called Pinseeker. All this was before 1980, when he set up Riley Golf. John was more of a creator and less of a marketer. Jim Flood, the other highlighted innovator, tended to be more extreme, but very creative. He started by setting up the original graphite shaft company, Aldila, in 1971. Before Aldila really got under way, he had sold out and was on to other interests. One was the "Basakwerd" putter and another the "Power Pod" driver. He started Odyssey putters, but again was off to other things before that got going. It is people like Jim Flood that make this business so interesting for all of us and that made it so challenging for the USGA and Frank Thomas.

In the early '70s, Ram's business had grown to the point that new shipping facilities were needed. A building of 150,000 square feet was constructed with large shipping docks and office space in Elk Grove Village near O'Hare airport. This location became the new corporate headquarters and provided the space needed for the large international shipments that Ram was now doing.

The site of the US Open in 1970 was Hazeltine National Golf Club in Minneapolis. This was a new course that some of the players were not too pleased with. This was especially true with Ram staff member, Dave Hill. Dave was a Vardon Trophy winner and played on three Ryder Cups so when he criticized a course it was serious. Several of the pros disliked the blind shots to hidden greens and the many doglegs. During an interview, Dave said the course was missing "only 80 acres of corn and a few cows to be a good farm." This did not sit well with tour management and a locker room meeting was scheduled for Dave with Joe Dey, Commissioner of the Tournament Players Division of the PGA of America. As Joe Dey walked in, the locker room became very quiet as everyone strained to hear what was coming. Joe said "Dave, I am going to have to fine you $150." Dave's only reply was "Is that all?" Joe just took Dave's response in stride and left without comment.

Joe was a very distinguished gentleman and had formerly been the executive director of the USGA. He was the first tour commissioner after the Tournament Players Division had become a separate entity in 1969. Upon Joe Dey's retirement in 1974 he was replaced by Deane Beman who was instrumental in changing to the current name of PGA Tour. Deane also was successful in leading its dramatic growth in the '70s and on into the '90s.

Dave Hill would later write a book that included a discussion with Deane Beman about why golfers tend to be conservatives, in which he quoted Deane: "Golfers are conservatives because they have a real sense of value about working at a profession and getting back what you put into it. There are no shortcuts in golf. It's a dead honest game. You're entirely self-sufficient. You don't rely on anybody, but yourself. You have to police yourself. There is no fudging the way there is in football or basketball where a player tries to grab an opponent's shirt to slow him down. Golfers have a great advantage over the average guy. You can't kid yourself. You have to have the ability to accept failure, whether you're an unknown rookie or Jack Nicklaus. For all the bright clothes, golfers are very down-to-earth people."

One of the entertaining highlights of US Open history occurred at the 1971 US Open at Merion Golf Club near Philadelphia. The day after regulation play, Jack Nicklaus and Lee Trevino met for an 18-hole playoff. The scene is a very staid group of USGA officials and two of the all time nice guy professionals. This is when Lee reaches in his bag, pulls out a rubber snake, throws it at Jack and the two of them burst out laughing. With this, Lee broke the ice and most around joined in, although not so much with some of the officials. Lee prevailed that day with a 2-under par round to be the 1971 US Open champion with the snake back in the bag.

After oldest Hansberger brother Bob had established himself in Boise, Idaho he found time to start a new business that fit the beautiful wilderness country that was a part of Idaho. He acquired the resort called Mackay Bar and then brought brother Al and myself in as partners. This back country resort included a landing strip along the Salmon River and an abandoned gold mine called the Painter's Mine. The Salmon was known as the "River of No Return" popularized by the 1954 movie of the same name with Marilyn Monroe and Robert Mitchum. The area was so remote that there was no road access and two Cessna 206 aircraft were acquired to transfer guests to and from Boise. Activities included jet boating, whitewater rafting, steelhead fishing, backpacking and hunting. The area was home to bear, mountain lion, bighorn sheep, mountain goat, wolves, elk, moose, and mule

Dave, Scott, and Jim Hansberger

deer. Elk hunting became a family tradition and the brothers and sons found time for the fall hunt almost every year for 30 years. A large house was built overlooking the river that was used by both Boise Cascade and Ram for company meetings. The house was called, of course, "The Ram House."

With all the time the brothers and their families had spent in the Idaho back country, the idea of what the Australians would call a "walkabout" sounded interesting. One of my four children was chosen to take the time off from summer activities and the trip was scheduled for July 1976. The two of us, father and 14-year-old son, Dave, were flown out of Boise to a landing strip in the Salmon River Wilderness at about a 5,000 foot elevation. From there we took off with backpacks and hiked up a

9,000 foot mountain. We were alone and only carried a limited supply of freeze dried vegetables with the intention of "living off the land." We did exactly that and walked out of the mountains six days later well fed and in good shape having covered over 65 miles with a lifetime of experiences. When our ancestors settled this land, they did not have Holiday Inns or McDonalds and got along just fine. It helps build a young man's self confidence to know that it can still be done.

"...The messy and long running litigation between Ping and the USGA was a bit unique, because that was over the issue of USGA rules and the interpretation thereof."

CHAPTER 8

Shock and Possible Disaster

The future looked bright for Ram in 1972. The golf ball side of the business was doing especially well because of the success of the Surlyn-covered ball. DuPont had agreed to delay offering the unique Surlyn formula that Ram had developed, and sales were continuing to grow. The Golden Ram ball was showing tour wins, and more pro shops were carrying the product.

Then it happened. The company received a cease and desist letter from Dunlop Golf in England saying they had obtained a US patent, and the Ram golf ball was infringing. We were innovators and engineers. We were not legal experts, and like many entrepreneurs we had not thought about patenting our developments. Now we had to study patent law and obtain legal help. It turned out patent law was different in England than in the US. In England patents are awarded on the bases of "first to file" while in the US it was on first to use or, "prior art." The choices for Ram were:

a) Accept the Dunlop position and stop making the product that was now one third of the company business.

b) Prove "prior art" by showing that Ram or others had produced and publically distributed the product prior to the Dunlop filing date.

c) Look to a possible license with Dunlop.

We decided that our position was strong enough that the company would have a good chance of defending our rights. There also was a strong feeling of "justice" because by this time Ram had made and sold millions of Surlyn-covered balls and Dunlop had sold none. If, however, Ram lost, it would be very likely that Ram would not survive. Dunlop filed suit and the battle was on.

Terry Pocklington and I, along with attorneys Herman Hersh and Ted Scott, started extensive investigative work. We found that Clem Wittek of the Wittek Range Supply Company of Chicago had been associated with a small golf ball company in California that had made balls with durable covers. Ted and I then traveled to California and soon found evidence that the Metropolitan Golf Ball Company had indeed made balls with Surlyn covers. There were further indications they had tested them with various Hollywood celebrity golfers including Bing Crosby as early as 1964, but how could it be proven? The answer would have to lie with L B Wagner who had been the CEO/Owner of Metropolitan. The problem was he had died in 1965. He did however have a daughter that handled his estate. When contacted, she acknowledged that he had a safety deposit box with his papers. Ted and I asked that it be opened and examined. It was found to contain a dated Surlyn formula in L B Wagner's handwriting that preceded both Ram and Dunlop dates.

Dunlop still persisted in going forward in the trial in Chicago Federal District Court. After a long drawn out trial with much evidence being presented, Judge Parsons ruled in Ram's favor. Dunlop appealed and the appellate court again ruled for Ram. Dunlop still would not give up and filed a Petition for "Writ of Certiorari," which is a request for the case to be heard by the Supreme Court. The Supreme Court denied the Petition, which meant after years of litigation Ram was vindicated and survived.

The golf industry has become a very litigious industry regarding patents. There tended to be two types of lawsuits. The first is similar to the Dunlop/Ram suit above. This was where one company would be trying to protect its trademarks and patents from competitor infringements. There were many examples of this, including the multiple suits between Spalding and Titleist over golf ball patents. Most of these would be settled, but only after a lot of attorneys' fees. In approximately 1980, Ram was accused of infringing on a Spalding golf ball patent. At the time a company in Taiwan that we were operating was negotiating a contract to supply the Spalding "Executive" wood golf head. An amicable arrangement was worked out whereby a large quantity of heads was supplied to Spalding at a reduced price and the potential suit was dropped. Everyone walked away a winner.

Another example of this was the dispute between Callaway and Ram. Ram had manufactured a club called the Accubar that used a mark referred to as a "Chevron." This is the same arrow design that Callaway in 1991 started using on the top of their metal woods (Big Bertha, etc). As the popularity of the Big Bertha grew many "knock offs" from China and Taiwan started showing up at US customs. Since all these copies carried that Chevron logo, the solution by Callaway was to register the Chevron mark and then use that as justification for US customs to stop the infringing products. When they went through the registration and enforcement process, Ram said you can't do that because that is our mark. A settlement was worked out where Ram sold their rights to Callaway and Callaway was then successful in obtaining a registration and being able to control much of the infringement. Callaway still uses that mark on their products and as a part of their corporate logo.

The messy and long running litigation between Ping and the USGA was a bit unique, because that was over the issue of USGA rules and the interpretation thereof.

Rather than a company protecting their own product there are cases where an individual pursues a golf company over possible patent infringement. The individual finds some product being made by a small company that has not been widely distributed. He then applies for a patent on some feature in its construction. Years later when a similar product is being marketed by a larger golf company, he threatens them with a lawsuit. Even though the validity and/or enforceability of the patent are questionable the golf company will frequently decide that it is less costly to pay the antagonist something to go away, than to pay attorneys to defend it.

An example of this was Tony Antonious. Over the years, Antonious made a profession of chasing golf companies using various patents. Many in the industry would consider them questionable at best.

One patent was on the Velcro closure on a golf glove. In the '70s Antonious was able to obtain cash settlements from several in the industry. When he approached Ram, we were able to show products made prior to his questionable patent and, rather than risk his successes with other companies, he left Ram alone. Joe Phillips of Wilson was quoted as saying this about Antonious "Sure I remember when we settled with him. You want to know my opinion? He just patented everything in sight, whether he invented the product or not. He let anybody use Velcro, and then after they were successful he said: 'I own that patent, you owe me royalties.' He was very intelligent, and he knew how to play that game."

Antonious also came up with several patents on weight distribution on irons and Barney Adams, founder of Adams Golf, had this to say, "How can anybody patent weight distribution in an iron? We (golf club manufacturers) have been distributing and redistributing weight forever and ever."

Over the 50 years spent in the golf business, I have been involved in many legal proceedings, both directly as a participant in lawsuits and as a witness. I have had the good fortune to work with some of the best attorneys in the legal field and would like to make special mention of patent attorneys Herman Hersh, Ted Scott, and Jim Ryther and also business/corporate attorneys, Chuck Rubin and Doug Walter.

More golf club companies were emerging in the Chicago "cluster." Gary Adams, who was a salesman with Wittek Driving Range Supply in Chicago, was involved in selling metal woods to driving ranges.

In 1979, he came up with the idea of making metal woods for regular play and then started a company called TaylorMade in McHenry, Illinois. Later Gary ran out of money and the company was sold to Adidas and moved to Carlsbad, California. Gary was not out of ideas however and founded McHenry Metals. Again, he ran into money issues and that company folded. Gary was still not done, and started Founders Golf in 1991 which was sold to a Japanese company in 1996. Gary was one of the innovators of golf, but was never fully able to take personal advantage of his own creativity.

With several companies moving and/or starting there, southern California in the '80s was becoming a new "cluster" for club making companies. Titleist was already there and other companies starting club operations in Southern California included Cobra Golf, Cleveland Golf, Callaway, and Lynx Golf.

CHAPTER 9

Ram Joins Colgate

The Hansberger brothers sold Ram Golf to Colgate Palmolive in 1974. It was a bit unusual for a major international household products company to get into a specialty business like golf. There were, however, some good opportunities that Colgate wished to pursue. Colgate products were purchased primarily by women, and golf was becoming more and more popular with ladies. The Colgate plan was to become a major sponsor of the LPGA and to sign as many lady professionals as possible to endorsement contracts. Colgate would then use them in advertising for Colgate household products.

The driving force behind this move by Colgate was the President and CEO David Foster. David was an Englishman, who had been a lieutenant commander in the Royal Navy. He loved the sport and played as often as time permitted. The first step in his plan was to buy a golf company. His only problem was there were none available. After doing some research he homed in on Ram Golf and prepared an offer to the Hansberger brothers. The proposal was very favorable but, with the four brothers being very happy with the way the business was developing, the Colgate offer was declined. David Foster, however, was not to be deterred and a new offer, the proverbial "offer that could not be refused," was presented. With the price settled, the major sticking point became the non-compete agreements that Colgate was requiring. As a part of this, Colgate was offering employment contracts to the brothers. The brothers decided, however, that they would prefer no non-compete and no employment contract. This was accepted by Colgate with a gentlemen's agreement that the brothers would not compete and would stay with the company for two years. After that there would be no restrictions on either party.

Over the next couple of years, many PGA Tour and LPGA golf professionals were added to the Ram staff. On the men's side, there were Tom Watson, Gary Player, Jim Dent, Seve Ballesteros, Curtis Strange, Nick Faldo and Peter Oosterhuis. They joined players that had been on the staff previously including Tommy Bolt, Doug Sanders, Bob Rosburg, Tom Shaw, Gene Littler, Ray Floyd, and Dave Hill. Players that joined the staff later included Nick Price, Peter Jacobsen, Mark Brooks, Calvin Peete, and Cesar Sanudo. Ram had the distinction of having had a staff player that would become a knight when, in 2009, Sir Nick Faldo became the only golf professional ever to receive such an honor.

On the ladies' side it was more of a Colgate/ Ram staff. This included Nancy Lopez, Jan Stephenson, Pam Barnett, Debbie Austin, Myra Blackwelder, Bette Burfeindt, Marlene Hagge, Marlene Floyd, Pam Higgins, Kathy Hite, Joyce Kazmierski, Joyce Deese, Sally Little, Susie Maxwell Berning, Debbie Meisterlin, Mary Mills, Pat Bradley, Mary Bryan, Kathy Postlewait, JoAnn Washam, Silvia Bertolaccini, Amy Alcott, Jane Blalock, Joann

RAM ADVISORY STAFF MEETING 1978
Gary Player, Jim Hansberger, Ron Howell, Bob Rosburg, Gene Littler, Tom Watson, Marlene Hagge, Al Hansberger, Judy Rankin

Prentice, Sandra Palmer, Sandra Post, Maria Astrologes, Kathy Ahern, Kathy Cornelius, Donna Caponi Young and Judy Rankin. Later, Patty Sheehan joined as well. This was an exceptionally strong staff, and one that only Colgate could afford. About 25 lady players and 15 men was a number that far exceeded the company's ability to take advantage of the endorsement opportunities. Over the company's entire history, Ram had over 80 different touring players on staff, but never as many at the same time as during the Colgate years. An example of the Ram staff domination of the ladies' tour at this point was at the Colgate Dinah Shore tournament in Palm Springs, California in 1976. Of the top 10 on the leader board, eight were Ram staff members.

David Foster and Colgate were very successful in connecting with the LPGA tour to promote Colgate products. The Colgate Dinah Shore tournament, which was held each year, received major television exposure after its beginning in 1972. The LPGA had been struggling and the Colgate sponsorship, national television and a large purse gave a huge boost to women's golf throughout the '70s. Hall of Famer Judy Rankin became a close friend of David Foster and was quoted as saying, "It is somewhat forgotten what a big part he played in the rise of the LPGA in the '70s. Much of what the players are enjoying today goes back to his vision."

Carol Mann, another Hall of Famer, recalled, "David fell in love with the LPGA players and was committed to treating them like stars. He convinced Dinah Shore to become the tournament's host and she invited her celebrity friends to participate. Foster's support sustained the LPGA during the 1970'. For nearly a decade, David Foster was the LPGA's patron saint."

From 1975 thru 1978, Al and I participated in the Colgate Dinah Shore tournament each year. This was Colgate's opportunity to fully show their class and entertain customers. It was a gala affair and the dinners and parties were exquisite. Each five-person group in the ProAm included a tour player, a Colgate host, a celebrity, and two Colgate customers. Al and I participated as the Colgate hosts in our respective groups. During this time with Colgate, our celebrity partners included Bob Hope, Lawrence Welk, Dinah Shore, Ray Bolger, and Gary Morton.

These people were all great to play with and always spent time after playing enjoying conversation. Bob Hope was a very enthusiastic player and always ready to make the people laugh. On one par 5, Bob hit his ball over the green and as he got ready to hit his chip he made some gesture that made the quite large gallery start laughing. He stopped and with his deadpan look he said, "No, you laugh after I hit." This wound the gallery up even more. His wife, Dolores, joined after the group finished and charmed all of us.

Lawrence Welk was a character and had a lot of ladies following him, which he encouraged. His game was so-so, but he definitely was enjoying the audience. Dinah Shore had just joined Hillcrest Country Club in Los Angeles and had started taking lessons from Eddie Merrins of Bel-Air Country Club. Eddie went along to help with Dinah's game. Just having him along was a big help to Dinah's confidence. She was a great spokesperson for the tournament and seemed to love being the official hostess. Ray Bolger, who played the "Tin Man" in the Wizard of Oz was a natural comedian and a great partner. Gary Morton was the second husband of Lucille Ball, and an avid player and comedian that kept the group in good humor.

Many of the LPGA players were signed by David Foster himself with little participation by Ram. Thus some of the women players were more beholden to Colgate than to Ram. Even though the contracts they signed stated they would play Ram equipment exclusively, a few felt little obligation to do so. The normal procedure for a new signing would be for the player and the manufacturer to work together over about a one to three month period as the player adjusted to the new equipment. During this time, the clubmaker would be making all the necessary fitting modifications. This obviously requires cooperation. Any change in equipment requires a positive effort by a player to adjust.

Ram experienced a bit of a problem at this time, best explained by the following story. During the Colgate Dinah Shore tournament in 1976, at the Mission Hills Country Club in Palm Springs, California, I was summoned to come over to the David Foster house, not far from the first tee. There were several Colgate executives there along with three of the lady professionals that Colgate had signed. David was holding court and was a bit "in his cups" (British term). David had been having a discussion with the players about their getting Ram clubs into their bags as the contracts required. These three professionals were telling him that Ram just did not know how to make clubs that fitted their requirements. David turned to me and said "Jim, you will just have to make some changes so you can fit these ladies. Let's not rush them into new clubs until they are ready." The end result is they never were "ready" and their contracts were not renewed.

David had a keen British sense of humor. While watching the groups teeing off, it was observed that one of the Colgate customers in a group had a large and impressive new staff bag. The player took a swing and as the ball dribbled down the fairway, David quietly said, "He's all bag."

It was often felt that the assimilation of Ram by Colgate would have made a great study by the Harvard business school. There were many pros and cons in the relationship. On the negative side was the fact that almost every other week a new executive from Colgate would show up from New

York to visit the operations in Chicago. Since Ram did not have any spare executives to handle this, it became the responsibility of either Al as president, or me, as VP of Marketing, to be the tour guide and chauffeur. Colgate also wanted to control the advertising, which required that either Al or I had to be at the New York Park Avenue headquarters of Colgate almost every other week. At first, we would stay in New York long enough to take in dinner and a play, but that got old very quickly. We would then arrive in New York in the late evening, go to the meetings during the next day and leave as soon as possible to return to Chicago, so we might even get back early enough to go into the office that evening to get some work done.

The Ram/Colgate relationship was an unusual arrangement. They were such different types of businesses that there really was no division into which Ram fit. Ram, with perhaps 20 million in sales at that time, basically was at the same organizational level with Colgate divisions of 500 million to a billion or more in sales. We were therefore reporting primarily to David Foster himself and to Dick Vail, the Colgate CFO. There was a good working relationship, but the respective numbers each worked with were dramatically different.

On the positive side, Ram/Colgate had assembled a fantastic tour staff. Tom Watson alone won 39 PGA Tour tournaments, with the first being the Western Open at Butler National in Chicago in 1974. His wins include five British Opens, the Masters twice, and the US Open. He was player of the year and/or leading money winner 11 times

RAM ADVISORY STAFF MEETING 1979
Marlene Hagge, Ray Floyd, Bob Rosburg, Tom Watson, Gary Player, Nancy Lopez, Terry Pocklington, Judy Rankin, Lyle Hansberger, Gene Littler

and after Ram, when he had joined Adams Golf, Tom added 13 Senior wins that included five Senior majors. Let's not forget his almost winning the British open again in 2009 at the age of 59. Tom's manager, Chuck Rubin, became close personal friends with all of us at Ram, and Chuck joined us on many hunting trips and proved his capabilities with elk, pheasants, turkeys and even the exotics in Africa. Chuck also managed Lee Trevino. Jay Sigel was a premier amateur and a long time player of Ram irons. Jay won the US Am, the British Am, the US Mid Am and was on nine Walker Cup teams. Chuck took over the management of Jay when he was ready for the Senior Tour in 1994.

"...Players who have won the World Cup representing the United States include Sam Snead, Ben Hogan, Arnold Palmer, Jack Nicklaus, Johnny Miller, Lee Trevino, and Tiger Woods."

Paul Svanberg, Tom Watson and Jim Hansberger with two of Ram's European Distributors.

CHAPTER **10**
Settling in to the Colgate Family

A huge plus from Colgate was a dramatic strengthening of Ram's international business. Colgate had relationships throughout the world and they introduced Ram to every country in which golf was played. In most cases, through their connections, they set up local distributors who introduced Ram to the local retailers. The very impressive tour staff made this easy for them to do. Within a few years, there were Ram distribution centers in 32 countries. Colgate also established personal relationships for my brothers and me on a worldwide basis. A big contribution of Ram's European distribution was Ram's CFO, Paul Svanberg. Paul was a native of Latvia and because of the War, Paul had lived in Russia and in Germany where he had worked with the US consulate. It seemed he could speak many of the European languages and this and his knowledge of European markets was a big help. Paul was so energized by the opportunities in Europe that he relinquished his CFO duties to Ron Schram and took on the European market full time.

During this period, Colgate bought several other golf-related companies, including multiple companies in England and one company in Australia. They then set up a new Colgate

International Golf Division and put my brother Al Hansberger in charge. This was in addition to his ongoing responsibilities as president of Ram. Ram became distributors for several Colgate-related products from England including the Penfold ball and Morton Knight rainwear. One thing the British knew how to do well was to make great golf rainwear! Ram also became the US distributor for the Swedish made Tretorn golf shoe.

Al and I were invited to participate in the World Cup which was held at Palm Springs, California in 1976. Our partners in the ProAm were Ram staff member Seve Ballesteros and his Spanish team member Manuel Pinero. Seve was only 18 at the time, and would go on to win the Masters two times and the British Open three times, along with many other victories. Seve was known as a bit of a handsome charismatic rogue and women loved him. The World Cup is a prestigious international event in which a two-man team is chosen to represent each country. Players who have won the World Cup representing the United States include Sam Snead, Ben Hogan, Arnold Palmer, Jack Nicklaus, Johnny Miller, Lee Trevino, and Tiger Woods.

During the Western Open in 1976, Ram staff member Cesar Sanudo stopped in to the Ram plant to be fitted with a new set of clubs. Cesar knew exactly how he wanted the heads ground and he knew how to do it. He went to work grinding a set of Ram "Tour Grind" iron heads. These were the forged carbon steel type that most tour players were using at that time. After Cesar left, the heads were finished, plated, assembled to his specs and shipped to him. When Cesar first took them to the range, his close friend Lee Trevino was there and asked to try them. Lee "borrowed them" for that tournament and a few more, several of which he won. Ram sent Cesar a new set with the "Sanudo Grind" which became the requested grind for many of the Ram staff. Players that went on to win with the special Sanudo Grind after Lee Trevino included Tom Watson, Nick Price, Mark Brooks, Jay Sigel, Peter Jacobsen, Calvin Peete, Ray Floyd, Nancy Lopez, and Patty Sheehan.

In 1977, an event occurred that became known as the "Duel in the Sun." After two rounds at Turnberry, Tom Watson and Jack Nicklaus were tied for the British Open lead. They entered the fourth round still locked in a tie after each shooting 65 in the third round. The battle went all the way to the end as Jack shot a great round of 66 and still lost to Tom's closing birdie for a 65. This was also known as "The Tournament of the Century" and showed the young 26-year-old Tom Watson was the new gun in town.

UPS became a major force handling small shipments in the late '70s. They could get a package from point A to point B very quickly and at a reasonable cost. This was perfect for a set of clubs or a case or two of balls. UPS had obtained the rights to handle shipments throughout the US in 1974. This was called the "Golden Link" and meant that Ram and other golf companies were able to close their costly extra shipping locations. Ping was one golf company that jumped on the UPS bandwagon and by the '80s Ping became a major UPS customer.

Business slowed in the late '70s. These were the years of the Carter administration with gas lines and 18% interest rates. Golf became a luxury item that few could afford, a very good example of how politics affects everything, even golf. It would appear that not many business people, golfers or not, would have been very happy with having Carter as their president. This was a period of golf courses, golf retailers, and golf manufacturers all experiencing very tough times.

In the late '70s, Karsten Solheim decided to take Ping into the golf ball business. A lot of money was invested and a good playing golf ball was developed. Karsten was creative in making the balls in two colors but, as successful as he was in the putters and irons, the ball business just did not work for them. After a good 10 years of effort he decided there was too much competition. This project could very well have been a success if it had been done at a different time. This did demonstrate that in the golf business you seldom find a company that is capable of being a market leader in both balls and clubs.

CHAPTER 11

Leaving Colgate

By mid 1977, Al and I were becoming more uncomfortable with the direction that Colgate was taking Ram. We both felt Ram was being used more to support Colgate marketing than for its own development. Unable to give Colgate our full support, we felt it was time to move on. We asked Colgate management to send out whomever they chose for replacements and we would do whatever we could to help with the transition. The relationship with Colgate was always good so there was no problem with this and it was agreed for us to stay on up to three months. We finally left in September of 1977 with no regrets. Brother Lyle, who by this time was running his ranch and the golf ball operation in Pontotoc, Mississippi decided to stay on. The manager that Colgate sent in was a good man, but without any golf background his learning curve was heavy and slow.

Within a few weeks after leaving Colgate, Al and I set up a new company called Hansberger Golf Products. At this time, there was an increasing move throughout the golf industry to have iron heads cast and polished in Taiwan. The Carter administration (1977-1981) created a huge problem for manufacturing businesses and increased the competitive pressure to move labor-intensive jobs overseas. We joined with Keith Knox of Australia, who had also sold his company to Colgate, to establish another new company called Phoenix Wood Products in Kaohsiung, Taiwan.

This was in a new tax-free export processing zone where the businesses were primarily Australian, Japanese and American. In this new plant, raw laminated maple heads were imported from the Birchwood Company in Wisconsin and Persimmon wood from the Far East. Phoenix began the process of making wood golf heads to customers' specifications so that finished wood heads could be imported ready for assembly. This mirrored the finished iron heads that golf manufacturers were already importing. With the connections and relationships we had in the industry, we were soon supplying products to many US golf companies including Spalding, Wilson, and Cobra. Customers in Japan, England and Australia were also established. The Taiwan plant quickly became very busy during this late '70s and early '80s period. One of the products was the Cobra "Baffler," which became a major success for Cobra. The "Executive" club was also a very successful product for Spalding. These were both products of Phoenix. It was believed that by this time nearly 70% of the world's total golf heads were being processed and finished in Kaohsiung, Taiwan and the surrounding area.

The new company did, however, require much management time. It was blessed to have Fred Wu, a former Taiwanese Naval Officer as company manager. Also there was Barry Giles, a former employee of Keith Knox in Australia as plant engineer. Al, Keith Knox, and I were experienced golf people so at least one of the three tried to be there a part of every month. This plan worked well and there were relatively few problems.

I ended up spending quite a bit of time there. For exercise and relaxation I joined a jogging club called the "Hash House Harriers." The route usually was close to the "beautiful" Love River. (The jogger could tell he was close by the smell.) Thankfully, the Love River has since been cleaned up. The club was mostly expats, especially Australians. It worked like this: A couple of guys would lay out the trail with clues of some sort. In some cases, the trail would go through a store and in one case it was arranged with some locals to leave the front door of their house open so the runners could run in and then out through the back door. The object was to find the "Stash" which was, of course, Taiwan beer! Runners that could not finish had to run the next event holding a toilet plunger. The extent of my mandarin was, "Wawong dai fong du," supposedly, "Take me to the Kingdom Hotel." This seemed to get a taxi driver to take me to the right place.

During my time in Taiwan, I became very impressed with the Taiwan education system. The son of our general manager was Johnny Wu. Johnny had taken the very tough college entrance exam in Taiwan and had not passed it. He then spent three years in the Taiwan military and then again tried unsuccessfully to enter college there. His father, Fred, then asked if I would help Johnny. We brought him to Chicago and entered him first in a language program to improve his English. From there he was able to enter North Park College in Chicago. Within three years he had his undergraduate degree with almost perfect grades and then received his MBA from San Jose State in California. It says something about the comparison of the two education systems when an individual does not qualify for the Taiwan college program, but proves to be an above average student in the US system. Johnny is now a successful business owner in California.

The late '70s had become quite competitive, especially in golf balls. Some companies came up with "creative marketing" and there was no greater example than Spalding's "The longest ball" campaign. The buzz in the industry was that In order to prove their claim they tested driving distances between their two-piece Top Flite and the wound balata Titleist and found the Top Flite to be about 10 yards short, so that did not work. They then had both men and women hit drives, took an average, and came closer. Next they had half the shots hit with irons and came still closer. Finally they added high handicap players who topped many of their shots. When they did this on the soft cover Titleist, the ball cut and did not go very far, but the cut proof Top Flite still ran a good distance on a "skulled" shot. By taking an average, sure enough, Top Flite was the longest ball. The ads then carried the line that read "when tested with average golfers, both men and women, hitting both woods and irons, Top Flite is the longest ball." How's that for being creative?

There was an increasing business with individual clubmakers who would buy finished heads and then assemble them and custom fit their customers. To take advantage of this market, Al and I established the Diamondhead Golf Company in

Bensonville, Illinois. This company would import stock golf heads from our Taiwan company and provide inventory that was available on short notice for these clubmakers. Our various startup companies seemed to have bright futures except for a new development in late 1979 that changed everything.

"...The Colgate executive said Colgate had decided the golf business was no longer for them and, were we interested in buying Ram back?"

CHAPTER 12

Return to RAM

Sometime in mid- to late 1978 the board of directors of Colgate decided it was time for David Foster to go. The board selected Keith Crane, a native of Australia, as the new President. Keith was a good businessman whom we knew well through various meetings at Colgate headquarters in New York. A month or two after the change we received a call from New York. The Colgate executive said Colgate had decided the golf business was no longer for them and, were we interested in buying Ram back?

We got together and decided, yes, if the price is right we would. This time it would just be three brothers, Lyle, Al, and I. Bob, the former chairman of Ram, who had retired from being president of Boise Cascade, and had formed a new company called Futura Corporation, would only be in an advisory capacity. The new executive team was planned out. Lyle, who was the original president, would be VP of Golf Ball Operations, Al who had been the president under Colgate would be VP of Sales and Marketing, and I, who had been VP of Manufacturing and then VP of Sales and Marketing, would be president. In effect, my brothers decided it was to be my turn in the hot seat.

After a few more meetings with our corporate

attorney, Doug Walter, we scheduled a meeting at the New York, Park Avenue headquarters of Colgate. As we waited outside the meeting room, I noticed there were a half dozen or more Colgate executives in the room, but only two of us. This made me a bit uncomfortable but, Doug, who was used to this type of meeting, was reassuring and the meeting went well. Within a reasonable period of time, an agreement had been reached on the basic terms and price. When Ram was sold to Colgate back in 1974, it was an all stock transaction. We wanted to buy it back on the same basis, but Colgate said no, this deal has to be for cash. For tax reasons, selling our Colgate stock at this time was just not practical. The price was favorable at less than the original sale, but raising this much cash would be a challenge. Because of this cash issue, the transaction was put on hold with an answer due within a week.

The negotiating team headed back to Chicago to proceed to the next step. The family had prior connections to a major Chicago bank and immediately contacted their head man of business lending. A meeting was held and after we explained all the details and background, the banker announced that he thought the plan was sound and he would submit the proposal to the bank's business loan committee. The banker said we should have an answer within a week or two. We were not comfortable with that answer so we headed to American National Bank, also in Chicago. There we met with Norm Bobbins who was the bank's chief officer for business loans in the Midwest. The same background was presented to Norm and after a few questions and answers he said "Okay." We then said our problem is we have to get back to Colgate right away. He said, "I already gave you my answer." That began a Hansberger family/ Ram Golf banking relationship with American National Bank and Norm Bobbins that lasted many years. It had been a vote of confidence that would never be forgotten. American National Bank later was acquired by LaSalle National Bank and Norm Bobbins later became the president and then chairman of LaSalle. That was a man that knew how to make timely banking decisions.

The next step was to prepare the agreements, which was a pretty big job for the lawyers. The final agreement required an inventory and analysis of the inventory. That raised some differences of opinion. After the inventory was complete, a meeting was held in Chicago with the Colgate accountants. One issue was the unbalanced sets of golf heads. Colgate wanted the same value on unmatched numbers as on matched sets of heads. It had to be explained that irons were sold in sets, so unmatched 3 irons, for example, have little or no value. There also was an old inventory of golf gloves and thin cabretta leather deteriorates over time. The explanation was made for a reduced value with no success until the non- golfing accountant decided to put on one of the gloves in the inventory. When he did so, the glove tore in half. The point was made and the rest of the valuation negotiations went more smoothly.

During the discussions, we explained to Colgate that there was no way Ram could take over all the tour player contracts that Colgate had negotiated.

It was decided that Ram would retain the contracts for Tom Watson and Nancy Lopez. Ram thus had the leading money winners on both the LPGA and the PGA Tours. Most of the other contracts were left with Colgate and they then had the responsibility of buying them out. Ram did add several other pros later, but it was done on the basis of what would work best for Ram.

Most of the international distributors were kept in place and that provided the opportunity to develop the international business in a major way. The details were finalized and on December 28, 1979 Ram Golf was back with the Hansberger family. The relationship with Colgate had been very good and both parties held up their respective ends of the bargain. Ram Golf was a much stronger company than when it was sold in 1974. This was true even though the company showed a loss in its last year under Colgate. We had every confidence that Ram would be back in the black in 1980. The company was in debt, but the opportunity was there. It was now up to the family again and we were happy to be back.

CHAPTER 13

RAM Under New Management

There was much to do and it was important to do things quickly. The returning owners needed to reassemble the team. Al and I were back taking over the overall management with Lyle handling the golf ball manufacturing operations in Mississippi. With him was Terry Pocklington, Ram's talented golf ball engineering manager. In the corporate headquarters in Melrose Park, Illinois, Ram had the very capable Gary Diehl, the marketing manager that Colgate had brought in. Jerry Fortis and his advertising agency joined, and soon became a major part of the team. Bob Lukasiewitz was the experienced golf club plant manager who had a great staff of engineering and manufacturing professionals. It was a huge advantage that most of the original team was still on board so there was not a people problem. What was missing was direction and planning. There also was a needed emphasis on new product development.

Another help at that time was the positive publicity Ram received because of the Hansberger family returning to the golf scene. We were frequently interviewed and articles were being written in major publications about Ram. These articles appeared in the Wall Street Journal,

Executive Golfer, Golf Magazine, Golf Digest, Golf World, Chicago Tribune, Chicago Sun Times, and sports pages throughout the country.

Golf World is the weekly golf publication where golf companies run their win adds to publicize staff victories. Ram had such a winning staff that, over the years, hundreds of Ram win ads were run. Golf World asked Ram to participate in a letter for its own advertising campaign. The following letter printed in Golf World in March of 1980 is an example of the industry support that was received.

"THANK YOU!   IT'S GREAT TO BE BACK......AND WITH GOLF WORLD, "SAYS RAM'S PRESIDENT, JIM HANSBERGER

"To the many of you golfers and golf professionals who have called or written to welcome Lyle, Al and me back to Ram, special thanks.

In contemplating the repurchase of Ram, we've given a lot of thought to future marketing plans. It was and is increasingly clear that our future in this highly personal business is with the devoted golfer and his golf professional. It's these "regulars" and golf professionals and assistants at almost every club who read GOLF WORLD religiously. It's also these regulars who will be playing golf next year and beyond and who will continue to be somebody's good customer.

Even with a Tour staff like ours, that includes Tom Watson and Nancy Lopez, it would be difficult and costly to effectively reach our customers and good prospects without

GOLF WORLD. I hasten to add, we just do not believe expensive mass marketing and TV techniques are the answers .... there is more to this personal business than numbers and more numbers.

Personal service is something devoted and professional golfers appreciate and something I would like to think GOLF WORLD and RAM have in common. Yes, it's great to be back, and that includes back with GOLF WORLD."

We felt it important to create a family atmosphere for our men's and women's staffs and our company personnel. The players' needs were our priorities and the players visited our plant at least once a year to get new clubs to replace their worn-out ones.

Jim, Al and Scott Hansberger with Dick Taylor, Editor of Golf World circa 1982

They also attended company meetings. When it came to making forged clubs, Ram was the head of the class. We had very experienced craftsmen who knew how to grind a club head to a specific weight, make it look good to the eye of our discerning players, and it played as well as it looked.

We invited our players to a grinding seminar at our Melrose Park plant and Tom Watson, Calvin Peete, Patty Sheehan, Peter Oosterhuis, Peter Jacobsen, and Sandra Post all accepted. They met with John Brisk, Ed Gorski, Joe DiPrizio, and Howie Davis of our custom department staff headed by Chuck Taft. It was a great learning experience for all participants. Peter Jacobsen ground a complete set of irons, and had a ball doing so. When he finished he proudly showed them to head grinder, John Brisk. John looked at them and asked the important question: Did you put a shaft in and look down at the club head as if you were addressing the ball? When this was done Peter realized he had ground so much of the club that it was no longer playable. Peter response was, "I'm going back to playing golf; you grind the clubs." The rewarding part of this session was that these great players all learned how to communicate their needs to craftsmen that could make exactly what they wanted. They also got a genuine understanding of how complicated it is to make a set of golf clubs correctly.

Ram's incredible staff kept winning. Calvin Peete became leading money winner and Vardon trophy recipient in 1984 and he became known as "Mr. Accuracy." Calvin had the never to be matched record of being the leader in fairways hit on the PGA Tour for 10 straight years, 1981 to 1990. Nancy Lopez had 48 tour victories and was named player

CALVIN PEETE

of the year four times. Working with the very best players helped Ram develop better playing equipment and helped in Ram's reputation as a premier equipment maker.

Recently, Calvin reflected on his time with Ram. "I had a relationship with Ram before I ever had a contract. I had gotten a set of Ram Tour Grinds when I was trying to play the mini tour in Florida. I loved the clubs. I was stuck on Ram clubs long before I qualified to play on the PGA Tour."

"Ram's Tour Grind was the best club because they had professional people who knew how to grind a good golf club. It just wasn't pretty. It felt good and it played even better. I liked to have a special bounce on the irons and they could do it right every time. I could trust that there was no lead down the hosel to make it right. It was pure. I won 11 times in the '80s and Ram Golf was a major reason for my success."

"Being on the staff with Tom Watson, Peter Jacobsen, Peter Oosterhuis, Sandra Post, and Patty Sheehan made me feel special. The Hansbergers and the tour rep Gary Diehl were very good friends, not just a friendship based on a contract."

"The Ram Golf family was first class! The company was first class! And their products were second to none!"

Over the next few years, Ram developed many new products. The Tom Watson 3-wedge system was very successful. The chip-in by Tom on the 17th hole at Pebble Beach to win the US Open in 1982 was a big marketing tool to sell wedges.

Ram worked with Dr. Joe Braly of the Precision Shaft Company to develop the methods needed to manufacture clubs using the "frequency matched" system. Joe had been trying to market his shafts and system for some time, but without too much success. Ram was able to make frequency matching viable and practical for top line clubs.

The way Ram became convinced that frequency matching had merit was through a tour player by the name of Jimmy Jamison. When he came into Ram's custom club department, his set of irons was carefully examined. The Ram clubmakers asked, Why do you have two MacGregor clubs, three Hogan clubs, two Wilson clubs, and two Spalding clubs? Jimmy explained that he had spent hours selecting clubs out of different sets on a basis of feel. When they were put through the testing gauges they were found to be a perfectly frequency matched set. Jimmy had frequency matched his set entirely by feel. That was a pretty good indication that Dr. Braly was on the right track and the commitment was made to proceed. From there on all Ram top line clubs became frequency matched and thousands of sets were sold using Braly's shafts.

Most irons at that time were forged and required skilled craftsmen to grind the proper shape while maintaining the correct weight required for frequency matching. Several shaft and grip companies had started to provide a trailer at tour stops so pros could have their clubs reshafted and regripped. When the technicians on these trailers took players clubs apart it was found that most of Ram's competitors were shoving lead weights down the shaft to correct their lack of skill in grinding. When they took Ram irons apart they found the heads had been ground to the proper weight so no extra weights were necessary. That was a key reason Ram was more successful than others with the frequency matching process. Later the basic "FM" system was used by all the top brands and today virtually every tour player and low handicap golfer is being fitted through this basic concept or system.

Another product concept that was developed by Joe Braly was the "Featherlite" club. This consisted of reducing the head weight so that the swing weight would be in the B8-C2 range instead of the standard D2-D4 range. Two of the early users of Featherlite clubs were Ray Floyd and Tom Kite. Ram had a trademark for the name Featherlite and marketed its version under that name. Many other companies started making their versions as well, but under different names. The exception was a company started by Dave Pelz in Austin, Texas that was named Preceptor Golf. Dave had resigned from his position as a senior scientist with NASA in 1976 to go into the golf business. In 1982, Dave started marketing his club under the same "Featherlite" name and Ram issued a cease and desist letter. The two companies were not able to settle the disagreement and ended up before a judge in the Federal District Court in Brooklyn. The Judge was so bad that in the middle of the trial he announced that he was going to suspend the trial because "he needed to wash his car." He also announced that many who came before him in trials would like him to retire, but "they could not get rid of me because I was appointed for life." When he did hand down a decision it was basically meaningless and solved nothing. The Preceptor Golf Company was dissolved in 1986 and Barney Adams, who had been working for Dave, bought the assets. He then used them to start the company now known as Adams Golf. Since that time, Dave has become a very successful expert, teacher and writer on the short game.

CHAPTER 14

Zebra Putter Joins RAM

Back in the '70s, Bob Rosburg, who was on the Ram staff, introduced Ram to Dave Taylor, who had developed a putter called the Zebra using the concept of "face balanced." This involved putting a special bend in the shaft and then distributing the weight in the head of the putter so that the face would be perfectly flat when allowed to balance. This had the effect of the face remaining square to the hole through the stroke. Included in the design were adjustable weights and Zebra stripes on top for alignment.

Ram made an arrangement with Dave whereby his company called Taylorcraft would manufacture the Zebra, and Ram would handle the sales and distribution. This worked fine initially, but the Taylorcraft manufacturing facilities were so limited that it was little more than an accessory to Ram. Through the Colgate years, because of limited availability and since the patents and trademarks remained with Taylorcraft, there was little incentive for long term marketing.

As the '80s began, with the Hansbergers back, new attention was given to the Zebra. Shortly after Dave Taylor passed away in the early '80s all marketing rights, patents and trademarks, dies and fixtures were purchased by Ram from his son Dale.

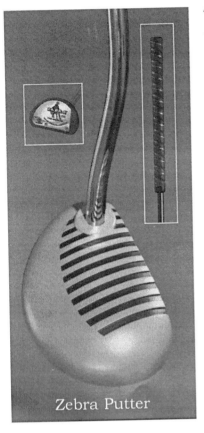

Zebra Putter

The Zebra already was in the hands of many touring professionals due to the efforts of Bob Rosburg. Now it just needed the manufacturing and marketing, and Ram did just that. Hundreds of thousands of Zebra putters were made and sold at a retail of $70 each, which was higher than most of the competition. Gene Littler had won the Crosby at Pebble Beach in 1975 for the Zebra's first win. Arnold Palmer was also an early user. Thereafter into the '90s the Zebra probably showed up in every pro tournament and had many, many wins. A very memorable win was Nick Price sinking a 50-foot putt with his Zebra to win the British Open in 1994. In 1992, Nick had won some tournaments with a Ray Cook putter that was similar in shape to the Zebra, but without the stripes. Ray Cook then starting running ads saying "The Zebra Has Lost Its Stripes." Since Nick was on the Ram staff, it was a bit embarrassing and Nick quickly changed to the Zebra.

The golf ball business was developing well also

and with Terry Pocklington, Ram was continuing to make a better and better product. The first win for the Golden Ram golf ball had been by Ram staff professional Tom Shaw in 1971, also at Pebble Beach. Tom Watson soon won with the Golden Ram ball and Tour Staff players Calvin Peete, Peter Jacobsen, and Patty Sheehan posted wins as well. Those wins gave Ram more credibility in the pro market which historically had been dominated by Titleist. They initially told the pros that only the Titleist method of making a soft synthetic balata cover could produce a tournament quality ball. Titleist claimed the Surlyn cover Golden Ram was not acceptable for tournament play. Titleist kept saying that up to the point that the Ram success was such that they had to convert to blends of Surlyn for their own cover. From that point on, Ram's ball sales still grew, but at a slower rate.

A conflict developed between Ping and the USGA in 1985 concerning the grooves in the Ping Eye2. The grooves in the face of the irons had historically been V shaped when stamped into the face of a forged iron. By 1985, many of the clubs being made

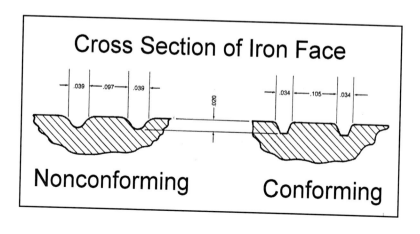

Cross Section of Iron Face

Nonconforming   Conforming

were cast and the casting process was more flexible in the type of groove that could be produced. In 1984, the USGA had changed the rules to allow square grooves. The second version of the Ping Eye2 was then brought out in 1985 with square grooves that had slightly rounded edges into a U shape. This made the grove a tiny bit wider at the surface than the rule specified. The players using the Ping Eye2 U groove wedge on tour seemed to get a little more backspin which the players using V groove wedges objected to. The disagreement came down to how the measurement was made. The long time technical director of the USGA was Frank Thomas and he and Karsten Solheim did not agree on the measurement and as a result Ping ended up suing the USGA. This battle went on for some time to the detriment of Ping, the USGA, and the industry. Finally, John Solheim convinced his father that the matter needed to be settled and a reasonable settlement was agreed to. This allowed the Ping Eye2 to be grandfathered for a period of time. As of 2010, all irons had to be manufactured to the USGA measurement. This way both parties won.

CHAPTER 15

Emphasis On Marketing

The golf business was becoming more competitive in the '80s and so there was a greater effort by all the golf companies to develop better ways of marketing their products. The largest professional tournament is the National Club Pro Championship. In 1981, it was scheduled to be held at the new PGA National Resort in Palm Beach Gardens, Florida. This was such a large tournament that it required three courses for the 360 participants. Ram was invited by the PGA to become the tournament sponsor. The decision at Ram was that it would be a good opportunity to further develop on-course presence for the company. The sponsorship amount requested was $150,000 which seemed reasonable.

The tournament went well and Ram signed up for a second year, but this time the requested amount had moved up. When the tournament was moved to LaQuinta, California and the amount increased yet again Ram reluctantly agreed to a third year. Ram's justification was the success they had in encouraging many of the club pros to use the Golden Ram ball in the tournament.

With Ram's success, other ball companies sent their representatives to promote their products. Titleist was especially aggressive in trying to discourage players from using the Ram ball in the

Ram-sponsored tournament. Ram felt the PGA officers did not make sufficient effort to make the tournament sponsor-friendly so when for year four, the PGA of America requested another escalation, Ram declined. The two PGA officers that did have the best understanding of the business side of golf were Don Padgett and JR Carpenter. During their respective two-year terms as president, they both showed a commitment to golf and to the golf professionals they represented. Don was instrumental in Ram's initial involvement and JR was the glue that kept Ram involved for three years in spite of the complications.

Ely Callaway had a successful career at Burlington Industries and then with a California winery. Instead of retiring after selling his winery, he started a third career in 1984 by buying a small company called Hickory Sticks. This little company was primarily making wedges with wood shafts. He soon changed the name to Callaway Golf and expanded into a line of clubs. Before long the company had several million dollars in unsold inventory with little interest by the market.

At this point, most small companies would have folded, but Ely was creative and came up with a plan. He was able to barter his unsold inventory for advertising space in both TV and print. He then acquired the design for an oversized metal-headed driver to be called the "Big Bertha." In effect, he ended up with an ad budget of 16 million dollars to achieve 8 million in sales and had enough barter dollars and his own cash reserves to make it happen. The Big Bertha initially had a lot of heads collapse and shafts break, but with good customer service and overpowering advertising, Callaway was able to dominate the big-headed metal wood market.

This very expensive, but successful marketing approach had a profound effect on the golf industry. So much so that some referred to the period before the late '80s as BC (Before Callaway) and after 1990 as AC (After Callaway). Many golf companies who had done well with an ad budget of 10% of sales BC were finding their sales slowing even when they increased that number to 15% or more. Prior to this time, many of the companies in the business were privately held and were contributing to the NGF to support golf. The non-golf corporations coming in, including Callaway, had little interest in industry support and the BC friendly golf industry was now AC and becoming dog eat dog, survival of the fittest.

By this time the investment cast irons from Taiwan/China were replacing the American-made forged carbon steel irons. This meant that the highly skilled craftsmen that companies like Ram employed were less and less needed. The change from persimmon woods to metal woods was having the same effect. No longer were golf clubs being manufactured using American craftsmanship. The US golf business was just becoming a case of assembling Chinese-made components. Callaway had the advantage of coming into the business as it was changing from a skilled manufacturing business to a marketing business of selling locally assembled imported components.

The change to an "AC" industry had a huge effect on a lot of formerly successful golf companies. Major golf companies that either disappeared or were swallowed up by corporate buyers included Hogan,

Lynx, H & B, MacGregor, Wilson, Spalding, and Cobra.

The PGA Tour with Deane Beman as commissioner was receiving more and more television exposure which was making the PGA Tour logo more marketable. The work that Deane did to take the tour to such a success level never seemed to be fully appreciated by many of the players. The team of Terry Diehl of PGA Tour marketing and Gary Diehl (not related) of Ram marketing put together a concept of Ram producing a line of golf clothing using the PGA Tour logo under license. The agreement was finalized in 1986 and resulted in many millions of dollars in clothing sales over the next few years. Products included shirts, hats, pants, jackets, shorts, socks, sweaters, vests, umbrellas and rainwear.

The design and sourcing for Ram was coordinated through Van Heusen with two new introductions per year. Most on-course shops primarily promoted their own course logo so country club sales were limited for the line. The off-course pro shops, however had no logo and so most did not offer clothing. The Ram line of PGA Tour golf clothing basically provided an entry into clothing sales for the off-course pro shop. It also sold well at many municipal courses.

The relationship between Ram and the PGA Tour was excellent in that both entities were run by business people and had common objectives. A special PGA Tour clothing staff was set up for players that did not have other clothing deals. It was a win win for everyone. Deane Beman and incoming commissioner Tim Finchem hosted conventions for licensees and associates in locations throughout

Deane Beman, Gary Diehl, and Jim Hansberger

the world. Examples were Barcelona, Spain and the Tryall Resort in Jamaica.

One of the great people on the Barcelona trip was Dr. Frank Jobe. Dr. Jobe had developed the Centinella Hospital rehab and exercise project that was part of the PGA Tour concept of strengthening players through proper training. A mobile fitness center was set up to be at each tour site for the players' use. Dr. Jobe's specialty was rotator cuff surgery on athletes. He basically developed the surgery and rehab methods that are common place today. His successful surgery patients include World Series pitchers Tommy John, and Orel Hershiser, and Super Bowl champion quarterback Jim McMahon. In November of 1992 he operated on Scott Verplank, who then went on to being chosen as a team member in the Ryder Cup and the Presidents Cup. The same morning he operated on Scott Verplank, Frank also put this author's rotator cuff back together.

"...In effect, a lot of Japanese "golfers" never play on a golf course. Golf course memberships trade on the stock market."

CHAPTER 16

Golf In Japan

The history of golf in Japan began in 1903 when the British built the first course in Kobe. It grew slowly until the late 1930s when war with the West became imminent. During the War years, the few courses became mostly military bases. After the War, golf came quickly back into favor and by 1976 there were over 1000 courses. The success of players like Jumbo Ozaki popularized golf in Japanmuch like Arnold Palmer did in the US. By 2010, golf courses had grown to 2400 and players to over 9 million.

Because of the cost of golf and the limited availability of courses, driving ranges came into the picture with over 5000 built, many of them triple deckers. In many cases, reservations were required to get a spot. In effect, a lot of Japanese "golfers" never play on a golf course. Golf course memberships trade on the stock market and golf in Japan was very much affected by the slow Japanese economy of the later '90s and on.

A round of golf in Japan is a bit different than what we are used to in the US. First, it is normally a long drive to the course or the trip to the course may be by train. Normally you will have a female caddy, who has your bag on a pull cart along with one partner's bag. After the first nine, you will have about one hour for lunch while waiting for your starting time for the second nine. When the round is finished, it is time for the Japanese bath. Obviously, this is an all day affair.

The golf business in Japan was booming in the late '80s and early '90s and it was a prestige thing to have US made clubs. Japanese businessmen liked to buy two sets of clubs. One set they would keep at their club and one set in their office to proudly show business associates the clubs they used. Clubs were expensive because of custom duties and the cost to belonging to a golf course was also costly. Golf in Japan and Korea was a very exclusive sport at that time. Companies that were very well positioned for the business there included Lynx, Ping and Ram. These three companies were the first to develop worldwide golf club distribution. All developed good organizations and regional managers that focused on Japan, Korea, Singapore, Hong Kong, Thailand and other golf markets in the Far East.

As the business in Japan grew, more US companies were bringing their tour staffs to Japan for exhibitions. In the '60s Gene Littler and I were involved in exhibitions in Japan and then in the '70s Tommy Bolt was invited on a Ram promotional tour along with Al Hansberger. Together they did exhibitions at driving ranges and golf courses in the Tokyo area. Tommy's swing was photographed and extolled repeatedly as the ideal for young Japanese players to learn. Tommy went on to win 15 PGA Tour events and was instrumental in the start of the Senior Tour, now known as the Chapions Tour. He was a very good friend of the Hansberger family and still kept in contact long after his playing days. Tommy passed away at the age of 92.

Nancy Lopez had joined the Ram staff in 1975 and in the mid-'80s joined with Al Hansberger on a promotional tour in Japan. Ray Knight, the Cincinnati Reds and New York Mets infielder, whom Nancy had married in 1982 was along and proved to be just as much of a draw with the Japanese press as Nancy. Every press conference had as many baseball writers as golf writers. It was one of the most successful promotional tours by any golf company staff ever in Japan.

Carl Ross, the President of Lynx, had done a marvelous job of marketing in Japan, but was not happy with the reputation of his distribution partner. Carl usually travelled with his beautiful Vietnamese wife Angie, but because of the expected issues she did not go with him on his trip to meet a new possible distributor. Carl flew unannounced to Tokyo to meet the potential partner. During the night at his hotel he received a phone call from the "problem" partner saying, "We know where you are." Carl was uncomfortable with the situation and decided "I am out of here" and was on the next flight back to Los Angeles. He felt much better negotiating from surroundings in which he had more control.

Carl was not the only one who had some distributor issues. Japan has an annual industry trade show quite similar to the US PGA show and it was well attended by US manufacturers. Ram's Japan distributor had arranged a press conference during the show in the early '90s to show off the Ram line to the Japanese golf press and to make me available for interviews. The preparations were well done with sushi and drinks for the large crowd. Right before the conference, the distributor announced to me and my wife Pola, who was traveling with me, that she would not be welcome at the press conference. Pola was a bit uncomfortable anyway having left our then 4 year old son, Tom, back in Chicago. Within about five minutes, Pola was on her way back to the hotel to pack her bags and there was no way to persuade her to stay. To add insult to injury, later I was to be presented with the entire bill.

Shortly after that, Ram set up a new distributor partnership called Ram Japan with a successful businessman named Mr. Tanaka . The relationship worked well and over the next few years Tanaka san and I played a good deal of golf together on both sides of the pond. Later, when the son of Tanaka san married, both Pola and I attended with Ram golf ball manager, Terry Pocklington and his wife, Joan. The wedding itself was a traditional Japanese wedding ceremony in a small chapel. The reception was an extravaganza with the golf business of Japan represented. For the Americans, it was the experience of a lifetime.

As the Far East business had become a more important part of the US golf companies' business, annual sales meetings were held in the area to show the latest products. Ram, for example, held these meetings in Guam, Hong Kong, and, of course, Japan. The meeting attendees would be from Australia, the Philippines, Thailand, Korea, Taiwan, and Singapore as well as the other countries mentioned above.

The Japan golf manufacturers such as Mizuno, Daiwa, Maruman, Endo, Honma, PRGR, and others were not happy that so much of the business was being taken up by American companies. A campaign began in which the local press and manufacturers publicized commentaries that only Japanese manufacturers knew how to make clubs for the shorter, lighter Japanese player. This did not have any bearing in fact, but the Japanese consumer tended to be nationalistic enough to believe it. Also as the economy slowed in Japan in the mid-'90s, Japanese golf manufacturers were fighting for their survival. All of the above contributed to a toughening of the Japan business for American manufacturers. About this time both Japanese golf manufacturers and automobile manufacturers made major moves toward exporting their products to the Americas and Europe. By the turn of the century, the domination of American companies in the Far East golf business and the auto business had lessened significantly.

More recently, golf in mainland China has grown rapidly. In 1994 there were fewer than a dozen courses, but by 2013 there are on the order of 600 courses. These courses are being designed by some of the internationally known designers like Nick Faldo and Jack Nicklaus, for example. In addition, thousands of driving ranges have opened. The rise of golf has been so rapid that the Chinese government has now put a moratorium on new construction. Most of the world's top players competed in tournaments held in China in 2013 at some of these new courses. Obviously, this becomes a whole new market for the golf industry as it has been for the auto industry.

"...It may have well been the largest international sales meeting in the industry in that a total of 31 countries were represented. The meeting was held in Chicago and then as all the participants traveled on to Orlando for the PGA show, a follow up session and golf tournament was held in Florida. How do you yell "fore" in 16 languages?"

CHAPTER 17

Europe and Other Markets

Although golf began in Scotland and spread throughout the British Empire, golf manufacturing never seemed to develop in the UK. Penfold and Dunlop were in the ball business for a time, but Penfold's business was limited and Dunlop became a Japanese company. American-made clubs dominated the market and most major US golf companies established UK divisions or distributors. Colgate had established a distribution structure with Martini and Rossi for distribution of Ram in England. When we returned in 1980, the question was how to go forward. The decision was made to arrange a meeting with the Martini and Rossi executives to consider Ram's purchasing their golf distribution division. I was in Hong Kong at the time and arranged to fly overnight to London for the meeting. By lunchtime, the agreement had been reached and some Martini and Rossi beverage was provided to seal the deal. The manager of the Ram/Martini and Rossi distribution operation had been Stuart Barber and he then became the manager of Ram UK. Stuart lived in a beautiful old house on the Royal St. George's golf course in Kent where several Opens have been played. His home had a unique history with an old Roman wall as a part of the house.

Ram, as other US companies did, proceeded to set up a European sales management team and scheduled sales meetings in Europe. Most of the meetings were held in England, but one meeting was especially memorable in that it was held in Paris and included a cruise on the River Seine. The participants representing Sweden, Finland, Germany, Belgium, Switzerland, and Holland as well as France, Ireland and the UK seemed to enjoy the dinner and French wine as we all floated past the Louvre in a glass-bottomed boat.

South Africa was also becoming a good golf market. The success of, native son, Gary Player popularized the game much like Jumbo Ozaki had in Japan. We were able to set up a new distributor in Johannesburg called The Pro Shop. As the South Africa business was growing it was decided in the early 80's it was time for a promotional visit.

I then set off on a South Africa Airlines flight from New York to Johannesburg. At that time the national airline of South Africa was not allowed to fly over any other African country because of apartheid. We therefore had to make a refueling stop on the Ile de Sol (Island of the Sun) in the Cape Verde Islands. After being on the ground for a short time the Captain announced that one of the radios had gone out and we would have to wait 24 hours for a replacement.

We were then informed that the 4 hotel rooms on the island would be taken by mothers with babies and the other 350 passengers on the 747 would have a choice of sleeping on the plane or sleeping on the beach. Virtually all of us headed for the beach where the liquor cabinet was opened and a crayfish feast was prepared by the natives. It was a party.

In an unbelievable example of what a small world it is, I struck up a conversation with a South African mining engineer who told me he had once been the mining director at a mine in Idaho. It turned out that, yes, it was the abandoned gold mine that my brothers and I now owned. How can you explain, two men, from different parts of the world, meeting on the beach in the Cape Verde Islands, off the coast of Africa, discussing their common connection with a gold mine in the Salmon River Wilderness of Idaho?

After a "restful" sleep on the beach our replacement radio showed up and we were on to South Africa. The rest of the trip was much more routine.

The largest international sales meeting Ram ever had occurred in 1991. It may well have been the largest international sales meeting in the industry in that a total of 31 countries were represented. The meeting was held in Chicago and then as all the participants traveled on to Orlando for the PGA show, a follow-up session and golf tournament was held in Florida. How do you yell "fore" in 16 languages?

Ram's custom department not only made custom-fitted sets for tour professionals and low handicap amateurs, but many dignitaries as well. In April of 1993, I received a phone call from the Embassy of Morocco in Washington stating that the Ambassador to the United States from Morocco was on the way to Chicago and wished to meet with me. When Abdeslam Jaidi arrived he presented a jeweled dagger as a gift and told me how much his

MOROCCO DAGGER

majesty loved his new Ram custom made clubs. With the dagger was a handwritten note from King Hassan II which read:

> "I thank you deeply. I shall be very enjoyed and my game more powerful."
> Rabat, April 1993,
> The first servant of Morocco, Hassan II

Carl Ross and the Lynx sales force also had an especially memorable sales meeting. Theirs was held in South Africa. Carl was a big game hunter with many trophies. A sales meeting surrounded by wild animals seemed an ideal setting to discuss the golf business.

The situation in Europe was similar to that in the Far East relative to the acceptance of the Japanese vs. American brands. Prior to the '80s,

American brands of autos and golf equipment were dominant. American car makers and clubmakers then began finding their labor and regulatory costs in the US to be making them less competitive. For these and other reasons, by the '90s the Japanese brands became more accepted in Europe just as they had in the Far East.

"...Sam Snead was well known for being one of the country characters of golf. One of his quotes was 'The only reason I even played golf was so I could afford to hunt and fish.'"

CHAPTER 18

Tour Players andCelebrity Players

The Ram Tour Grind irons had become very popular with tour players in the '70s, '80s and on into the '90s. Contributing to this was the success that Tom Watson was having with the clubs. In 1992, Nick Price and Tom had a conversation about clubs and Tom encouraged Nick to contact Ram. When Nick stopped in to the Ram plant, he and I got together and set up a two-year plan for Nick to use Ram Tour Grind irons and to be on the Ram staff. The following year, Nick won four tournaments including the Players Championship, the Vardon Trophy, was leading money winner and was named Player of the Year. In 1994, the second year of the agreement, Nick won six times including two majors, the British Open and the PGA Championship. He again was leading money winner and player of the year. The good news for Ram was Nick was now regarded as the best player in the world. The bad news for Ram was that the two-year contract period was up and it was time to renegotiate.

Late in 1994, I was contacted by John Bredenkamp who stated he was now representing Nick and asked for a meeting. When he came to the Ram offices, it was quickly apparent that the meeting would not go well. It was obvious that Nick's value had rocketed upward, but Bredenkamp was not only talking millions, but also a percentage of the company. He indicated he already had such an offer from a startup company called Atrigon. It seemed that Bredenkamp had no intention of making any arrangement with Ram and the conversation ended quickly. Later, it was publicized that the Atrigon project had failed. Still later, it was revealed in various publications that Bredenkamp had been involved in or at least accused of being an arms merchant for Iran, Iraq and Rhodesia/Zimbabwe. Bredenkamp's company, Masters International, had become agents for Ernie Els, Robert Allenby, Michael Campbell and David Leadbetter, but soon lost its clients.

The situation was disappointing for Ram because we had wanted to retain Nick who was recognized as not only one of the best players, but also a good friend. Nick was a very knowledgeable clubmaker in his own right and assembled many of his clubs himself. Nick later would become the very capable captain of the International team in the 2013 Presidents Cup matches.

Every golf equipment company tended to have a lot of celebrity amateurs. Having well known athletes playing your clubs is good publicity. The Chicago Bears and Blackhawks players especially seemed to be into golf and with Ram located in a Chicago suburb, it was a natural fit. Stan Mikita, Bobby Hull, and Jim Pappin of the Chicago Blackhawks were great hockey players and enthusiastic golfers as well. Stan even turned to golf after retiring from hockey and became a club professional. Bobby and Stan were part of the 1961 Stanley Cup Champion Blackhawks. A few years later, owner Arthur Wirtz

Mark Brooks, Tom Watson, Nick Price

and manager Tommy Ivan decided to present golf clubs as Christmas gifts to the team. Each player was custom fitted by Ram and each player received a tour bag in the red and black team colors and with his name and the Blackhawk logo. The uniformed players with their staff bags made quite a picture.

Wilson was more involved with the baseball and basketball teams in Chicago. They fitted out Michael Jordan who seemed to play golf everywhere. Michael was a great ambassador and often was able to get in a round of golf before the evening basketball game. He did this at home and on the road and he still would be ready to hit the court in top form. Johnny "Red" Kerr was a good friend of Ram during his career as player, coach and announcer for the Bulls. Ram did have a few baseball players including

Ernie Banks, Whitey Ford, Yogi Berra and Davie Johnson, but the hardest one to fit was left-handed pitcher Sandy Koufax. He had such exceptionally long fingers that multiple wraps of tape had to be applied under the grip to build it up sufficiently so that his fingers would not dig into his palms. Ram also had a top tennis professional on its "celebrity staff" with Ivan Lendl.

Bears coach Mike Ditka and Bears players Kevin Butler and Jim McMahon visited the Ram plant quite often and were all good golfers. Mike Ditka was first fitted in 1962 when he was playing tight end for the Bears. At that time the woods were made out of Persimmon. Since Mike had not played much golf at that time and was so strong he ended up bringing the shafts for the woods back in two weeks with just pieces of wood still attached. Mike, of course, retired from being a player to become a coach. When he returned to Chicago in 1982 as the Bears coach, he also returned to Ram and was by then a fine player and a member of the Bob-O-Links Country Club in Chicago. There was a lady supervisor, Barb Pettikas, in the Ram shipping department that had a great sense of humor and was very outgoing. One time, when Mike was visiting the Ram plant, Barb saw Mike sitting in one of the offices, went over and put an arm over his shoulder and said "Could I bear your children?" This was probably the only time Mike Ditka was ever speechless.

When Peter Jacobsen would stop in Barb and Peter would have to take a few minutes to exchange the latest jokes. Peter was a great entertainer and imitator of other players. Some of his favorites to imitate were Craig Stadler, whose nickname was

CHICAGO BEARS
Coach Ditka and Quarterback Jim McMahon

the "Walrus." Peter would fill his shirt with golf balls and then imitate Craig's swing. He also did Arnold Palmer and Jim Furyk very well. Anybody that spent a lot of time on tour and walked toward the practice tee would recognize each player from a distance just by his swing. That is what made Peter's imitations so entertaining in the golf community.

Peter formed a band in the mid 80's with Mark Lye and Payne Stewart called "Jake Trout and the Flounders". They were fantastic with Peter as the lead singer and they performed at many events. They also recorded two albums. Peter's career has included tournament management, televised golf shows, and tournament broadcasting with The Golf Channel.

One of the finest gentlemen to ever play the game is Phil Mickelson. Phil had an amazing college career at Arizona State where he won the NCAA Individual Championship three times. In 1990 he won the US Amateur Title, the first lefty ever to do so. This win qualified Phil to play in the 1991 Masters as an amateur and to stay in the uppermost room in the clubhouse, the "Crow's Nest." Just off the locker room at Augusta, there is a small dining area for use by players and guests. One early practice round morning I was having breakfast there when this wide-eyed 20 year old walked in looking for a seat for breakfast. I invited Phil over and found him to be the nicest and most enthusiastic young man you could meet. Today he may be more mature, but he is still the same all around good guy and in addition to his many other wins, he has won that Masters tournament three times. In 1992, I had the opportunity to award Phil the Ram/Golfweek trophy as Collegiate Player of the Year.

The Ram association with Tom Watson began in 1975 shortly after he won his first tournament,

Jim Hansberger and Phil Mickelson 1992

the Western Open at Butler National in Oak Brook, Illinois. The sponsor relationship with Ram lasted 22 years. There are very few relationships on tour that last that long. Sam Snead and Arnold Palmer with Wilson and Fuzzy Zeller with H&B were other long termers. Tom was and is a man of ethics and principle and a handshake with Tom is as meaningful as a written agreement. Tom's manager, Chuck Rubin, became a close friend of the Hansberger family and still is today. Chuck was best man at our wedding. With a Catholic bride, a

Protestant groom and a Jewish best man we believed we had the bases covered.

Tom and Chuck put together an annual sponsor outing at the beautiful Greenbrier resort in White Sulphur Springs, West Virginia. The dozen or so invitees came from all over the corporate spectrum. Sam Snead was the pro emeritus at Greenbrier and sometimes joined the group. Sam had a long history with the Greenbrier and always enjoyed seeing Tom. Sam was well known for being one of the country characters of golf. One of his quotes was "The only reason I even played golf was so I could afford to hunt and fish." Sam passed away in 2002 at the age of 90.

The two-day outing was always set up as a scramble with a bidding after the first day of play to see who was thought to be the most valuable potential contributor to the team for the next day contest. The whole gathering was a "loose" affair and just a lot of fun. On one occasion Tom offered to play the team's worst drive. That happened to be mine because I hit my drive under a pine tree. Tom went in under the tree and found a way to punch the ball out and over the green. He then pitched it back onto the green and sank the 20-foot putt for a routine par. Tom did say however that if he had to play Hansberger's drive all the time he would give up the game. Tom replaced Sam as the pro emeritus at the Greenbrier and they have found Tom to be a great ambassador.

Chuck also manages Tom's good friend Lee Trevino who, at Tom's suggestion, played Ram irons he picked up from Cesar Sanudo. In golf, everybody seems to be connected. Another example was the

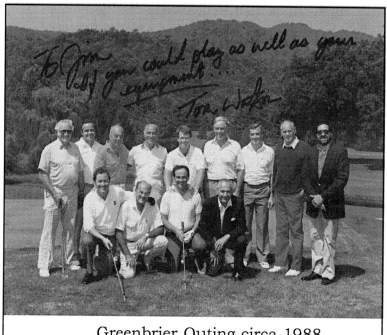

Greenbrier Outing circa 1988

13-degree Ram #3 metal wood that Fred Couples played. He got the club out of Tom Watson's trunk before Tom ever put it into play. That club received so much publicity that for two years Ram made as many #3 woods as drivers.

Over the years, two of Tom's most respected friends and mentors have been Byron Nelson and Sandy Tatum, who was his partner at the Crosby pro am for many years. Sandy was a great amateur golfer, and also served a term as President of the USGA. Byron not only acted as a swing coach, but a bit of personal mentor for Tom. Byron Nelson is a legend in golf, having won 11 tournaments in a row in 1945 and defeating Sam Snead and Ben

Hogan in those tournaments. He was known as Lord Byron because of his reputation as a gentleman.

As everyone knows, golf is a mental game and even more so for the professional. Once Jack Nicklaus was asked by a reporter what was he thinking when he was on the practice range hitting balls on the morning of the last day of the tournament. Jack's answer was, "I just wanted to find out who showed up." Tom Watson said one time, "If I can handle my bad shots well, I'm going to have a good day".

The sports psychologist that is best known on the tour is Bob Rotella. He has helped a lot of players learn to handle the ups and downs of tournament play. Rotella has worked with many players and two, for example, are Keegan Bradley and Darren Clarke. Dr. Richard Coop worked with Payne Stewart. Another person is this field is Julie Elion who has worked with Phil Mickelson.

Tiger Woods' father, Earl, made a lot of effort when Tiger was small to make him mentally tough. As an amateur, Tiger worked with Jay Brunza, a clinical psychologist, who was a friend of his father. Brunza also caddied for Tiger in many of his amateur tournaments. Tiger enrolled at Stanford after already having won the US Am. Earl Woods did not make the golf coaching job at Stanford very easy for my good friend, Wally Goodwin, and Tiger decided to turn pro after his second year. Gio Valiante, another sports psychologist has said that Tiger may have developed a feeling of entitlement which then creates added frustration when things don't go well. Valiante's students include Chris DeMarco, Bryce Molder and Matt Kuchar.

Tom Watson attended many promotional events for Ram over the 22 years he was on the team. He regularly stopped at the Ram tent at the British Open and signed autographs and talked to the customers. As a five-time British Open Champion, he always drew a crowd. One example of Tom's integrity took place in the early '80s. Most companies had a staff for either balls or clubs, but only a few of the companies required their staffs to play both the club and ball. Ram was one of those. Tom's contract was up for renewal and Ram was insisting that all staff members play the Golden Ram ball as well as the Ram irons. The Western Open was to be held at Butler National and Tom agreed to put the ball into tournament play for the first time and then meet with me after the first day's play at nearby Glen Oak Country Club for dinner and to wrap up the negotiations. The problem was that Tom came in with a score of about 4 over par. To say the least, I was uneasy with what Tom would have to say about the ball. That night the negotiations went well and the only thing Tom had to say about the day's round was, "I did not play very well today, but the ball played fine." Many players would have looked for an excuse, but not Tom.

No caddy/player relationship has ever been closer than Tom Watson with his long time caddy and friend, Bruce Edwards. The story was best told by John Feinstein in his book, "CADDY FOR LIFE." Bruce started caddying for Tom in 1973 when Tom was 23 and Bruce was 20. Greg Norman hired Bruce away in 1989, but then Tom hired Bruce back in 1993. In 2003, Bruce was diagnosed with Lou

Gehrig's disease (ALS) and the disease took his life in 2004 at the age of 49. Bruce was always pure golf and when he first told Tom what the doctors said he had, Bruce said "I made quad." That's tour terminology for quadruple bogey and it can't get much worse than that. Bruce also said "Well, at least my disease is named after a great athlete. I'd rather tell people I have Gehrig's disease than Liberace's disease." Bruce was one of the best liked caddies on the tour and Tom did everything he could possibly do to save or at least prolong Bruce's life. Their relationship was unique in that Bruce was much more involved in the decision making process during play than in most caddy/player relationships. The funeral was held in Ponte Vedra, Florida and the entire golf industry was well represented. The pallbearers were Tom and five of Bruce's fellow tour caddies.

In addition to the many tournaments Jack Nicklaus has won over the years, Jack has had many business involvements. He was the owner of MacGregor Golf for a period of time. His golf design company which is now run by his son Jackie has been very successful. Jack was the host for a small group of business associates at his beautiful house in West Palm Beach, Florida in the '80s. George Pepper, the Editor of Golf Magazine, and I were traveling together and were the first to arrive. Jack showed the two of us his many trophies and his valuable collection of George Low Wizard 600 putters while waiting for the other guests to arrive. It is also nice to have a yacht in your back yard. Wife Barbara and all five of the children were there as well. They are a beautiful family and Jack is a great family man.

One of the older gentlemen of golf that everybody admires is Errie Ball. He is the last living player from the inaugural Augusta National golf tournament, now known as the Masters. Errie celebrated his 90th birthday in North Palm Beach, Florida with many of his long time friends including Jack Nicklaus and the author. On November 14, 2010 a party was held at Willoughby golf Club in Stuart, Florida in honor of Errie's 100th birthday. Presenting the award was Bruce Patterson, golf professional at Butler National in Oak Brook, Illinois. Errie and Bruce had worked together at Butler for many years with Bruce as the head pro and Errie as the pro emeritus.

Errie Ball, Bobby Jones and two others circa 1936

"...One of the most faithful Christians on tour was Byron Nelson. It was said that it contributed to his calm demeanor which led to his descriptive title of 'Lord Byron.'"

CHAPTER 19

Religion on Tour

The golf industry will forever miss Karsten Solheim who passed away in the year 2000, 33 years after his founding of Karsten Manufacturing, better known as Ping. Karsten was a true innovator who became one of the most successful people the golf industry has ever known. Karsten and his family have always shown their strong Christian faith. The family sent an engraved Ping Anser to friends in his memory. This note was included with the putter.

There is a great mix of golf and religion on the

> *Please accept this commemorative putter in appreciation of your time and thoughtfulness following Karsten Solheim's homegoing. The engraving on the putter was one of Karsten's favorite Bible verses, Proverbs 3:5-6. We hope that you will cherish this small token of thanks as much as we cherished your heartfelt assistance as we celebrated Karsten's life and the joy of knowing he is now with our Heavenly Father, and our Lord, Jesus Christ.*
>
> *The Solheim Family*

Solheim Family Note

tour. Each Wednesday evening, a Bible study would meet, led by Larry Moody. Some of the regular attendees over the years include Paul Azinger, Steve Jones, Bubba Watson, Bernhard Langer, Davis Love, Tom Lehman, Larry Mize, Lee Janzen, Ben Crenshaw, Zach Johnson, Larry Nelson, Steve Lowery, Webb Simpson, Wally Armstrong, and Casey Martin. Tiger Woods has talked about being raised by a Buddhist mother and how his Buddhist faith has impacted his golf.

Steve Lowery gave talks about how his religion carried him through the trauma of having his house in Orlando burn down while he was at a tour event. His family was in the house at the time and miraculously escaped without injury. Casey Martin was granted an exemption to use a golf cart in tournaments, but only after litigation. His faith carried him through the many difficulties caused by the illness that affected his leg and limited his career. Casey had some amazingly good rounds in spite of his infirmity. One of the most faithful Christians on tour was Byron Nelson. It was said that it contributed to his calm demeanor which led to his descriptive title of "Lord Byron."

October 25, 1999 was a date of universal sorrow in golf. That is the date the Learjet carrying six people including Payne Stewart crashed in a field in South Dakota with no survivors. The plane had taken off from Orlando, headed for Dallas. Shortly after takeoff, it is believed the plane lost cabin pressure and without oxygen all aboard were incapacitated. The plane on automatic pilot continued to fly until it ran out of fuel four hours later. Payne had won the US Open for the second time, just four months earlier. Payne and his family were committed Christians and the funeral at First Baptist Church of Orlando had such a huge attendance that the ceremony had to be piped into other rooms at the church to accommodate Payne's world of friends. Christian artist Michael W. Smith performed a song he had written with Wes King. One verse goes as follows:

This was his time—This was his dance
He lived every moment—Left nothing to chance
He swam in the sea—Drank of the deep
Embraced the Mystery—Of all he could be
This was his time

PAYNE STEWART

"...David Feherty's knowledge of golf and his gift of interviewing in an interesting conversational manner has been a great add on to the Golf Channel programming."

CHAPTER **20**

Golf Channel Begins

The idea of a 24-hour TV golf channel was a unique concept of Joe Gibbs and Arnold Palmer. After much planning and investment, the channel opened January 17, 1995 in Orlando, Florida. Just a few weeks later the PGA Merchandise show was held at the huge convention center in Orlando. This is the national show that industry executives, sales representatives, and club professionals from across the country attend annually. It was a perfect time for the new channel to show off and they did. A number of industry people were invited to the studios for an introductory party. The founders, Joe Gibbs and Arnold Palmer, were there as well as Gary Player. The industry was represented by Wilson, Titleist, Spalding, Ping, Calloway, Taylormade, Ram, Adams and others. All were impressed with the state of the art equipment and the picture produced by all the HD digital cameras. HD was just arriving in TV broadcasting at this time which made the operation appear ahead of its time.

Later, the Golf Channel hosted golf outings in the Orlando area for their advertisers. One of these events was at the Mission Inn resort and included Arnold's flying in with his own helicopter to act as speaker and host. Since that beginning, partnerships have been formed with Comcast, NBC

Sports and the PGA Tour. Golf Channel has been a big success both for the founders and for the industry. A good part of that success is that they started off right and have constantly improved from there.

Jim Hansberger, Arnold Palmer, and Barney Adams

Golf Channel's commitment to golf made it the go-to place for companies to run their commercials and to do announcements of new products. Their broadcasting of the annual PGA show became a must see for the serious golfer. One of the special aspects of the station is its ability to do in-depth interviews with players and golf personalities. David Feherty's knowledge of golf and his gift of interviewing in an interesting conversational manner has been a great add on to the Golf Channel programming.

CHAPTER 21

Retirement Plans

The Hansberger family had been involved in the golf business for approximately 50 years. During that time we had started and operated golf and golf-related businesses in the US and throughout the world. The Ram headquarters had always been in Illinois and in 1997 my brothers and I were honored by our election into the IPGA Hall of Fame. At that time the following press release was issued:

Hansbergers Inducted Into IPGA Hall of Fame

Brothers Bob, Lyle, Al, and Jim Hansberger were inducted into the Illinois Section of the PGA Hall of Fame. The induction ceremony took place on October 8, 1997 at Oak Brook Hills Resort in Oak Brook, Il.

Each year the Illinois PGA Foundation recognizes those who have made major impacts on the game of golf, particularly in Illinois. The Hansberger brothers founded what is now the Ram Golf Corporation in 1947. Since that time, Ram Golf has developed many of the golf industry's milestone products and concepts.

"Innovation has always been the key to our longevity," said Ram Golf President, Jim

Hansberger. "The efforts and foresight of many people made this possible. The induction was an exciting moment for me and my brothers. We've done a lot of which we're very proud."

The Hansberger's family ownership of Ram Golf is unique on two counts. One. They've enjoyed the single longest family ownership in the golf industry. With all four brothers having an engineering background, Ram Golf has consistently enjoyed a position of leadership due to innovative equipment. Two. Ram Golf has been one of the few companies in the industry able to survive and flourish without the help of a public stock offering or the bankroll of a deep-pocketed company.

"We've always enjoyed a strong relationship with tour players as well as the club professional," says Hansberger. "You simply won't survive in this industry without the support of the golf professional. Likewise you won't garner their support without quality products."

Now into the mid-to late '90s. It was time to consider the dreaded word "Retirement." The company had been sold once successfully, but Colgate had not done especially well with it and Ram had been bought back and now it was bigger and better. However, the timing was not good. Every other major family-owned golf business, except Ping, had either been acquired, gone out of business or was on the way out. The corporate buyers had generally not had good success and

Al, Lyle, Jim and Bob Hansberger

that had the effect of reducing corporate interest in the golf business.

The industry was also in the AC mode as mentioned earlier. It was believed that, in order to keep up or move ahead in the industry under these circumstances, significant added investment would be needed. This would involve some risk and because of the desire of all of us to move into the retirement mode that would not seem to be a favorable option. The option that was finally decided on was to look at the four parts of the organization on an individual basis and to look at options for each.

The PGA Tour clothing line had been a very successful venture and the PGA Tour itself, under Commissioner Tim Finchem, had continued to grow. The tour was interested in licensing the name on many more products than clothing and on this basis

Ram had been approached about a buy back of the license which had now become quite valuable. A mutually satisfactory arrangement was negotiated that allowed Ram a phase out period and for the tour to start a licensing project on many other products. This also allowed Ram to sell the 75,000 square foot warehouse facility built to warehouse the clothing line. The company located next door to Ram was Alberto Culver and they welcomed the opportunity to expand their own warehousing operations.

In the 1980s the Hansberger brothers, along with Ram CFO, Ron Schram, had acquired a controlling interest in a computer software company in Rochester, NY. The company had been founded by Skip Toombs, a former executive with Eastman Kodak also in Rochester, New York. This company, Country Club Systems, provided the back office accounting systems for private clubs. Over the next few years CCS had managed to acquire two other companies in this specialized business and had become the largest company in the field with over 1,500 private clubs using its services. The company under Skip Toombs' continued management had expanded throughout the US and Canada and into other countries. Several companies were interested in an acquisition and in 1998 a very favorable negotiation was completed with Clubsystems Group.

The last two parts of the package were the ball operation in Pontotoc, Mississippi and the main office and club business in Melrose Park, Illinois. It was decided that the ball business and plant could be operated and sold independently and brother Lyle and brother Al took that responsibility. They were able to complete a sale to Taylormade and the Ram ball plant became the Taylormade ball factory.

Teardrop was a small putter company that investor Rudy Slucker had invested in and then bought out in 1996. In addition to the putter business, Rudy became involved in several developmental tours for aspiring golf professionals. Rudy had taken Teardrop public in late 1996. Then in 1997 he bought Tommy Armour Golf from US Industries. Tommy Armour had about 45 million in sales at that time, primarily in clubs, and US Industries had decided they wanted out of what had become the highly competitive golf club business. Rudy had also been negotiating an acquisition of the Ram club business and shortly after a deal was made to combine the manufacturing in the Tommy Armour, Morton Grove plant, about 15 miles from Ram. For the first time in over 50 years the Hansberger brothers would no longer be in the golf business.

After the transactions were announced, Teardrop stock increased in value and things looked very good for the new buyer. The combined sales for the first quarter of 1998 exceeded 25 million and were projected to reach the 100 million range for the year.

Teardrop started making some significant marketing efforts such as sponsoring a program on Golf Channel called the "Teardrop Putt of the Week" and also various other televised promotions. The problem was, however, Teardrop was fighting an uphill battle. Teardrop was trying to establish itself in a declining market. Total industry golf club sales ended up with a drop in 1998. It was an impossible situation without major financing and by 2000 it was over and the Teardrop company was in receivership. A classic case for Teardrop of: "How do you end up with 20 million dollars in the golf business?" Answer: "Start with 40 million."

It was disappointing for the Hansberger family to see the lack of success on the part of Teardrop, but once a company is sold, the commitment is made. Just as happened in the sale to Colgate in 1974 and the buy back in 1979, the buyback opportunity was there again in year 2000. This time, however, the market was much too soft, and Teardrop had harmed the Ram brand far too much. Also the decision to retire was still a commitment that was not going to change.

When the Teardrop sale was completed in early 1998 the Ram facilities in Melrose Park, Illinois were not included. There was a ready buyer again in the Alberto Culver Company next door who earlier had purchased the Ram/PGA Tour clothing warehouse. This became the most difficult transaction of all because the EPA had become all powerful in seeming to make things as miserable as possible for US manufacturing. The EPA believed if Ram had been doing metal finishing at this 104,000 square foot location for 40 years, Ram must have contaminated the soil and so numerous tests had to be made. Approximately $200,000 of make- work for bureaucrats later, the land was finally approved as safe and the sale could be finalized.

After retiring and moving south an opportunity arrived to be one of the volunteer golf coaches at the Trinity Prep School in Winter Park, Florida. Trinity Prep has an excellent golf program and is consistently one of the top teams in the area. Sam Saunders was an especially fine player who went on to playing the Web.com tour after completing his college career at Clemson. Sam also caddied in several Senior events for Arnold Palmer, who just happens to be his grandfather. This very fine young man looks to have a great future.

A nice touch was added when well after the brothers' retirement they again received an honor. The Hansberger brothers were the 2006 inductees into the Professional Clubmakers Society Hall of Fame. This took place on March 4, 2006 at the annual PCS awards dinner in Louisville, Kentucky.

The golf business and the US manufacturing business have gone through large changes over the last 70 years. I believe a simple sleeve of golf balls presently on the market can present an example of some of those changes. One of the first manufacturers of golf balls was the AG Spalding Co. in Chicopee, Massachusetts. In about 1969 they introduced the Spalding Top Flite golf ball. Today the Spalding factories in the US are closed. The name Spalding is owned by Russell Brands which markets many sports products made somewhere outside the US. The "Top Flite" brand has been separated from Spalding and is now owned by Callaway and the Top Flite ball sleeve reads "Made in Taiwan" in English and in Chinese. This one little sleeve of balls gives a mini inside picture of the changes in much of the golf industry.

Looking at the overall picture of manufacturing in America, we see that the golf business is just one example of what has happened and is continuing to happen. It is natural for labor intensive industries to move to the lowest cost, most business-friendly countries for their production. This has transferred the manufacturing of clothing, electronics, computers and many of the things we have in our homes, to overseas factories. Steel plants are closed and many of the Detroit auto factories have been shuttered. This situation obviously does not portend a long term positive future for the American economy and social structure.

The last 15 years has not been the easiest period for the golf business. However, since those first Scottish players were hitting their "feathery" down the fairway there has been many ups and downs and there will continue to be. The housing markets will improve and golf courses will be a part of that. Water restrictions will, however, be a limiting factor. Innovation has always been a part of golf and many more new products will be developed. The growth of golf in developing countries is a very positive sign for golf. The entrepreneur opportunities may not be as ideal as before, but the creative individual will still be able to find an opening. The playing of golf and the business of golf will continue to be with us for a long, long time.

This book has been written based on the personal experiences of the author. The golf industry is a unique industry and unique game that provides income, entertainment, exercise, and social relationships to millions. My family and I have been blessed to have spent our working lives with what I consider the classiest people on the planet. Golfers and the members of the golf community are good people and I am proud to have known and worked with so many of them.